EDUCATION AND THE HIGHER LIFE

First published 1900
This edition published by Lector House in 2024

ISBN: 978-93-6138-630-5

Lector House LLP
Registered Office: H. No. 96, Block C, Tomar Colony,
Burari, Delhi – 110084, India
info@lectorhouse.com
www.lectorhouse.com

EDUCATION AND THE HIGHER LIFE

JOHN LANCASTER SPALDING

2024

LECTOR HOUSE LLP

EDUCATION AND THE HIGHER LIFE

BY

J. L. SPALDING

Bishop of Peoria

The business of education is not, as I think, to perfect the learner in any of the sciences, but to give his mind that freedom and disposition, and those habits, which may enable him to attain every part of knowledge himself.—LOCKE

SIXTH EDITION

Contents

EDUCATION AND THE HIGHER LIFE.

Chapter I.

Ideals.

A noble aim,
Faithfully kept, is as a noble deed.

WORDSWORTH.

To few men does life bring a brighter day than that which places the crown upon their scholastic labors, and bids them go forth from the halls of the Alma Mater to the great world's battlefield. There is a freshness in these early triumphs which, like the bloom and fragrance of the flower, is quickly lost, never to be found again even by those for whom Fortune reserves her most choice gifts. Fame, though hymned by myriad tongues, is not so sweet as the delight we drink from the tear-dimmed eyes of our mothers and sisters, in the sacred hours when we can yet claim as our own the love of higher things, the faith and hope which make this mortal life immortal, and fill a moment with a wealth of memories which lasts through years. The highest joy is serious, and in the midst of supreme delight there comes to the soul a stillness which permits it to rise to the serene sphere where truth is most gladly heard and most easily perceived; and in such exaltation, the young see that life is not what they take it to be. They think it long; it is short. They think it happy; it is full of cares and sorrows. This two-fold illusion widens the horizon of life and tinges it with gold. It gives to youth its charm and makes of it a blessed time to which we ever turn regretful eyes. But I am wrong to call illusion that which in truth is but an omen of the divine possibilities of man's nature. To the young, life is not mean or short, because the blessed freedom of youth may make it noble and immortal. The young stand upon the threshold of the world. Of the many careers which are open to human activity, they will choose one; and their fortunes will be various, even though their merits should be equal. But if position, fame, and wealth are often denied to the most persistent efforts and the best ability, it is consoling to know they are not the highest; and as they are not the end of life, they should not be made its aim. An aim, nevertheless, we must have, if we hope to live to good purpose. All men, in fact, whether or not they know it, have an ideal, base or lofty, which moulds character and shapes destiny. Whether it be pleasure or gain or renown or knowledge, or several of these, or something else, we all associate life with some end, or ends, the attainment of which seems to us most desirable.

This ideal, that which in our inmost souls we love and desire, which we lay to heart and live by, is at once the truest expression of our nature and the most potent agency in developing its powers. Now, in youth we form the ideals which we labor to body forth in our lives. What in these growing days we yearn for with all our being, is heaped upon us in old age. All important, therefore, is the choice of an ideal; for this more than rules or precepts will determine what we are to become. The love of the best is twin-born with the soul. What is the best? What is the worthiest life-aim? It must be something which is within the reach of every one, as Nature's best gifts—air and sunshine and water—belong to all. What only the few can attain, cannot be life's real end or the highest good. The best is not far removed from any one of us, but is alike near to the poor and the rich, to the learned and the ignorant, to the shepherd and the king, and only the best can give to the soul repose and contentment. What then is the true life-ideal? Recalling to mind the thoughts and theories of many men, I can find nothing better than this, "Seek ye first the kingdom of God." "Love not pleasure," says Carlyle, "love God. This is the everlasting Yea, wherein all contradiction is solved; wherein whoso walks and works, it is well with him."

To the high and aspiring heart of youth, fame, honor, glory, appeal with such irresistible power, and appear clad in forms so beautiful, that at a time of life when all of us are unreal in our sentiments and crude in our opinions, they are often mistaken for the best. But fame is good only in so far as it gives power for good. For the rest, it is nominal. They who have deserved it care not for it. A great soul is above all praise and dispraise of men, which are ever given ignorantly and without fine discernment. The popular breath, even when winnowed by the winds of centuries, is hardly pure.

And then fame cannot be the good of which I speak, for only a very few can even hope for it. To nearly all, the gifts which make it possible are denied; and to others, the opportunities. Many, indeed, love and win notoriety, but such as they need not detain us here. A lower race of youth, in whom the blood is warmer than the soul, think pleasure life's best gift, and are content to let occasion die, while they revel in the elysium of the senses. But to make pleasure an end is to thwart one's purpose, for joy is good only when it comes unbidden. The pleasure we seek begins already to pall. It is good, indeed, if it come as refreshment to the weary, solace to the heavy-hearted, and rest to the careworn; but if sought for its own sake, it is "the honey of poison flowers and all the measureless ill." Only the young, or the depraved, can believe that to live for pleasure is not to be foreordained to misery. Whoso loves God or freedom or growth of mind or strength of heart, feels that pleasure is his foe.

> "A king of feasts and flowers, and wine and revel,
> And love and mirth, was never King of glory."

Of money, as the end or ideal of life, it should not be necessary to speak. As a fine contempt for life, a willingness to throw it away in defence of any just cause or noble opinion, is one of the privileges of youth, so the generous heart of the young holds cheap the material comforts which money procures. To be young is to be free, to be able to live anywhere on land or sea, in the midst of deserts or among strange people; is to be able to fit the mind and body to all circumstance, and to rise almost above Nature's iron law. He who is impelled by this high and heavenly spirit will dream of flying and not of hobbling through life on golden crutches. Let the feeble and the old put their trust in money; but where there is strength and youth, the soul should be our guide.

And yet the very law and movement of our whole social life seem to point to riches as the chief good.

> "What is that which I should turn to, lighting upon days like these?
> Every door is barred with gold, and opens but to golden keys."

Money is the god in whom we put our trust, to whom instinctively we pay homage. We believe that the rich are fortunate, are happy, that the best of life has been given to them. We have faith in the power of money, in its sovereign efficacy to save us not only from beggary, from sneers and insults, but we believe that it can transform us, and take away the poverty of mind, the narrowness of heart, the dullness of imagination, which make us weak, hard, and common. Even our hatred of the rich is but another form of the worship of money. The poor think they are wretched, because they think money the chief good; and if they are right, then is it a holy work to strive to overthrow society as it is now constituted. Buckle and Strauss find fault with the Christian religion because it does not inculcate the love of money. But in this, faith and reason are in harmony. Wealth is not the best, and to make it the end of life is idolatry, and as Saint Paul declares, the root of evil. Man is more than money, as the workman is more than his tools. The soul craves quite other nourishment than that which the whole material universe can supply. Man's chief good lies in the infinite world of thought and righteousness. Fame and wealth and pleasure are good when they are born of high thinking and right living, when they lead to purer faith and love; but if they are sought as ends and loved for themselves, they blight and corrupt. The value of culture is great, and the ideal it presents points in the right direction in bidding us build up the being which we are. But since man is not the highest, he may not rest in himself, and culture therefore is a means rather than an end. If we make it the chief aim of life, it degenerates into a principle of exclusion, destroys sympathy, and terminates in a sort of self-worship.

What remains, then, but the ideal which I have proposed?—"Seek ye first the Kingdom of God." Unless the light of Heaven fall along our way, thick darkness gathers about us, and in the end, whatever our success may have been, we fail, and are without God and without hope. So long as any seriousness is left, religion is man's first and deepest concern; to be indifferent is to be dull or depraved, and doubt is disease. Difficulties assuredly there are, underlying not only faith, but all systems of knowledge. How am I certain that I know anything? is a question, debated in all past time, debatable in all future time; but we are none the less certain that we know. The mind is governed by laws which neither science nor philosophy can change, and while theories and systems rise and pass away, the eternal problems present themselves ever anew clothed in the eternal mystery. But little discernment is needed to enable us to perceive how poor and symbolic are the thoughts of the multitude. Half in pity, half in contempt, we rise to higher regions only to discover that wherever we may be there also are the laws and the limitations of our being; and that in whatsoever sanctuaries we may take refuge, we are still of the crowd. We cannot grasp the Infinite; language cannot express even what we know of the Divine Being, and hence there remains a background of darkness, where it is possible to adore, or to mock. But religion dispels more mystery than it involves. With it, there is twilight in the world; without it, night. We are in the world to act, not to doubt. Leaving quibbles to those who can find no better use for life, the wise, with firm faith in God and man, strive to make themselves worthy to do brave and righteous work. Distrust is the last wisdom a great heart learns; and noble natures feel that the generous view is, in the end, the true view. For them life means good; they find strength and joy in this wholesome and cheerful faith, and if they are in error, it can never be known, for if death end all, with it knowledge ceases. Perceiving this, they strive to gain spiritual insight, they look to God; toward him they turn the current of their thought and love; the unseen world of truth and beauty becomes their home; and while matter flows on and breaks and remakes itself to break again, they dwell in the presence of the Eternal, and become co-workers with the Infinite Power which makes goodness good, and justice right. They love knowledge, because God knows all things; they love beauty, because he is its source; they love the soul, because it brings man into conscious communion with him and his universe. If their ideal is poetical, they catch in the finer spirit of truth which the poet breathes, the fragrance of the breath of God; if it is scientific, they discover in the laws of Nature the harmony of his attributes; if it is political and social, they trace the principles of justice and liberty to him; if it is philanthropic, they understand that love which is the basis, aim, and end of life is also God.

The root of their being is in him, and the illusory world of the senses cannot dim their vision of the real world which is eternal. By self-analysis the mind is sublimated until it becomes a shadow in a shadowy universe; and the criticism of the reason drives us to doubt and inaction, from which we are redeemed by our necessary faith in our own freedom, in our power to act, and in the duty of acting in obedience to higher law. Knowledge comes of doing. Never to act is never to know. The world of which we are conscious is the world against which we throw ourselves by the power of the will; hence life is chiefly conduct, and its ideal is not merely religious, but moral. The duty of obedience to our better self determines the purpose and end of action, for the better self is under the impulse of God. Whether we look without or within, we find things are as they should not be; and there awakens the desire, nay, the demand that they be made other and better. The actual is a mockery unless it may be looked upon as the means of a higher state. If all things come forth only to perish and again come forth as they were before; if life is a monster which destroys itself that it may again be born, again to destroy itself,—were it not better that the tragedy should cease? For many centuries men have been struggling for richer and happier life; and yet when we behold the sins, the miseries, the wrongs, the sorrows, of which the world is full, we are tempted to think that progress means failure. The multitude are still condemned to toil from youth to age to provide the food by which life is kept in the body; immortal spirits are still driven by hard necessity to fix their thoughts upon matter from which they with much labor dig forth what nourishes the animal. Like the savage, we still tremble before the pitiless might of Nature. Floods, hurricanes, earthquakes, untimely frosts, destroy in a moment what with long and painful effort has been provided. Pestilence still stalks through the earth to slay and make desolate. Each day a hundred thousand human beings die; and how many of these perish as the victims of sins of ignorance, of selfishness, of sensuality.

To-day, as of old, it would seem man's worst enemy is man. What hordes still wander through Asia and Africa, seeking opportunity for murder and rapine; what multitudes are still hunted like beasts, caught and sold into slavery. In Europe millions of men stand, arms in hand, waiting for the slaughter. They still believe, because they were born on different sides of a river and speak different languages, that they are natural enemies, made to destroy one another. And in our own country, what other sufferings and wrongs,—greed, sensuality, injustice, deceit,—make us enemies one of another! There is a general struggle in which each one strives to get the most, heedless of the misery of others. We trade upon the weaknesses, the vices, and the follies of our fellow-men; and every attempt at reform is met by an army of upholders of abuse. When we consider the murders, the suicides, the divorces, the adulteries, the prostitutions, the brawls, the drunkenness, the dishonesties, the political and official corruptions, of which our life is full, it is difficult to have complacent thoughts of ourselves. Consider, too, our prisons, our insane asylums, our poor-houses; the multitudes of old men and women, who having worn out strength and health in toil which barely gave them food and raiment, are thrust aside, no longer now fit to be bought and sold; the countless young people, who have, as we say, been educated, but who have not been taught the principles and habits which lead to honorable living; the thousands in our great cities who are driven into surroundings which pervert and undermine character. And worse still, the good, instead of uniting to labor for a better state of things, misunderstand and thwart one another. They divide into parties, are jealous and contentious, and waste their time and exhaust their strength in foolish and futile controversies. They are not anxious that good be done, nor asking nor caring by whom; but they seek credit for themselves, and while they seem to be laboring for the general welfare, are striving rather to satisfy their own selfish vanity.

But the knowledge of all this does not discourage him who, guided by the light of true ideals, labors to make reason and the will of God prevail. If things are bad he knows they have been worse. Never before have the faith and culture which make us human, which make us strong and wise, been the possession of so large a portion of the race. Religion and civilization have diffused themselves, from little centres—from Athens and Jerusalem and Rome—until people after people, whole continents, have been brought under their influence. And in our day this diffusion is so rapid that it spreads farther in a decade than formerly in centuries. For ages, mountains and rivers and oceans were barriers behind which tribes and nations entrenched themselves against the human foe. But we have tunneled the mountains; we have bridged the rivers; we have tamed the oceans. We hitch steam and electricity to our wagons, and in a few days make the circuit of the globe. All lands, all seas, are open to us. The race is getting acquainted with itself. We make a comparative study of all literatures, of all religions, of all philosophies, of all political systems. We find some soul of goodness in whatever struggles and yearnings have tried man's heart. As the products of every clime are carried everywhere, like gifts from other worlds, so the highest science and the purest religion are communicated and taught throughout the earth: and as a result, national prejudices and antagonisms are beginning to disappear; wars are becoming less frequent and less cruel; established wrongs are yielding to the pressure of opinion; privileged classes are losing their hold upon the imagination; and opportunity offers itself to ever-increasing numbers.

Now, in all this, what do we perceive but the purpose of God, urging mankind to wider and nobler life? History is his many-chambered school. Here he has taught this lesson, and there another, still leading his children out of the darkness of sin and ignorance toward the light of righteousness and love, until his kingdom come, until his will be done on earth as it is in heaven. To believe in God and in this divine education, and to make co-operation with his providential guidance of the race a life-aim is to have an ideal which is not only the highest, but which also blends all other true ideals into harmony. And the lovers of culture should be the first to perceive that intellectual good is empty, illusory, unless there be added to it the good of the heart, the good of conscience. To live for the cultivation of one's mind, is, after all, to live for one's self, and therefore out of harmony with the eternal law which makes it impossible for us to find ourselves except in what is not ourselves. "It is the capital fault of all cultivated men," says Goethe, "that they devote their whole energies to the carrying out of a mere idea, and seldom or never to the realization of practical good." Whatever may be said in praise of culture, of its power to make its possessor at home in the world of the best thought, the purest sentiment, the highest achievements of the race; of the freedom, the mildness, the reasonableness of the temper it begets; of its aim at completeness and perfection,—it is nevertheless true, that if it be sought apart from faith in God and devotion to man, its tendency is to produce an artificial and unsympathetic character. The primal impulse of our nature is to action; and unless we can make our thought a kind of deed, it seems to be vain and unreal; and unless the harmonious development of all the endowments which make the beauty and dignity of human life, give us new strength and will to work with God for the good of men, sadness and a sense of failure fall upon us. To have a cultivated mind, to be able to see things on many sides, to have wide sympathy and the power of generous appreciation,—is most desirable, and without something of all this, not only is our life narrow and uninteresting, but our energy is turned in wrong directions, and our very religion is in danger of losing its catholicity.

Culture, then, is necessary. We need it as a corrective of the tendency to seek the good of life in what is external, as a means of helping us to overcome our vulgar self-complacency, our satisfaction with low aims and cheap accomplishments, our belief in the sovereign potency of machines and measures. We need it to make our lives less unlovely, less hard, less material; to help us to understand the idolatry of the worship of steam and electricity, the utter insufficiency of the ideals of industrialism. But if culture is to become a mighty transforming influence it must be wedded to religious faith, without which, while it widens the intellectual view, it weakens the will to act. To take us out of ourselves and to urge us on to labor with God that we may leave the world better because we have lived, religion alone has power. It gives new vigor to the cultivated mind; it takes away the exclusive and fastidious temper which a purely intellectual habit tends to produce; it enlarges sympathy; it teaches reverence; it nourishes faith, inspires hope, exalts the imagination, and keeps alive the fire of love.

To lead a noble, a beautiful, and a useful life, we should accept and follow the ideals both of religion and of culture. In the midst of the transformations of many kinds which are taking place in the civilized world, neither the uneducated nor the irreligious mind can be of help. Large and tolerant views are necessary; but not less so is the enthusiasm, the earnestness, the charity of Christian faith. They who are to be leaders in the great movements upon which we have entered, must both know and believe. They must understand the age, must sympathize with whatever is true and beneficent in its aspirations, must hail with thankfulness whatever help science, and art, and culture can bring; but they must also know and feel that man is of the race of God, and that his real and true life is in the unseen, infinite, and eternal world of thought and love, with which the actual world of the senses must be brought into ever-increasing harmony. Liberty and equality are good, wealth is good, and with them we can do much, but not all that needs to be done. The spirit of Christ is not merely the spirit of liberty and equality; it is more essentially the spirit of love, of sympathy, of goodness; and this spirit must breathe upon our social life until it becomes as different from what it is as is fragrant spring from cheerless winter. Sympathy must become universal; not merely as a sentiment prompting to deeds of helpfulness and mercy, but as the informing principle of society until it attains such perfectness that whatever is loss or gain for one, shall be felt as loss or gain for all. The narrow, exclusive self must lose itself in wider aims, in generous deeds, in the comprehensive love of God and man. The good must no longer thwart one another; the weak must be protected; the wicked must be surrounded by influences which make for righteousness; and the forces of Nature itself must more and more be brought under man's control. Pestilence and famine must no longer bring death and desolation; men must no longer drink impure water and adulterated liquors, no longer must they breathe the poisonous air of badly constructed houses; dwellings which are now made warm in winter, must be made cool in summer; miasmatic swamps must be drained; saloons, which stand like painted harlots to lure men to sin and death, must be closed. Women must have the same rights and privileges as men; children must no longer be made the victims of mammon and offered in sacrifice in his temple, the factory; ignorance, which is the most fruitful cause of misery, must give place to knowledge; war must be condemned as public murder, and our present system of industrial competition must be considered worse than war; the social organization, which makes the few rich, and dooms the many to the slavery of poorly paid toil, must cease to exist; and if the political state is responsible for this cruelty, it must find a remedy, or be overthrown; society must be made to rest upon justice and love, without which it is but organized wrong. These principles must so thoroughly pervade our public life that it can no more be the interest of any one to wrong his fellow, to grow rich at the cost of the poverty and misery of another. Life must be prolonged both by removing many of the physical causes of death, and by making men more rational and religious, more willing and able to deny themselves those indulgences which are but a kind of slow suicide.

Never before have questions so vast, so complex, so pregnant with meaning, so fraught with the promise of good, presented themselves; and it can hardly be vanity or conceit which prompts us to believe that in this mighty movement toward a social life in harmony with our idea of God and with the aspirations of the soul, America is the divinely appointed leader. But if this faith is not to be a mere delusion, it must become for the best among us the impulse to strong and persevering effort. Not by millionaires and not by politicians shall this salvation be wrought; but by men who to pure religion add the best intellectual culture. The American youth must learn patience; he must acquire that serene confidence in the power of labor, which makes workers willing to wait. He must not, like a foolish child, rush forward to pluck the fruit before it is ripe, lest this be his epitaph: The promise of his early life was great, his performance insignificant.

Do not our young men lack noble ambition? Are they not satisfied with low aims? To be a legislator; to be a governor; to be talked about; to live in a marble house,—seems to them a thing to be desired. Unhappy youths from whom the power and goodness of life are hidden, who, standing in the presence of the unseen, infinite world of truth and beauty, can only dream some aldermanic nightmare. They thrust themselves into the noisy crowd, and are thrown into contact with disenchanting experience at a time of life when the mind and heart should draw nourishment and wisdom from communion with God and with great thoughts. Amid the universal clatter of tongues, and in the overflowing ceaseless stream of newspaper gossip, the soul is bewildered and stifled. In a blatant land, the young should learn to be silent. The noblest minds are fashioned in secrecy, through long travail like,—

> "Wines that, Heaven knows where,
> Have sucked the fire of some forgotten sun
> And kept it thro' a hundred years of gloom

Yet glowing in a heart of ruby."

Is it not worth the labor and expectation of a life-time to be able to do, even once, the right thing excellently well? The eager passion for display, the desire to speak and act in the eyes of the world, is boyish. Will is concentration, and a great purpose works in secrecy. Oh, the goodness and the seriousness of life, the illimitable reach of achievement, which it opens to the young who have a great heart and noble aims! With them is God's almighty power and love, and his very presence is hidden from them by a film only. From this little islet they look out upon infinite worlds; heaven bends over them, and earth bears them up as though it would have them fly. How is it possible to remain inferior when we believe in God and know that this age is the right moment for all high and holy work? The yearning for guidance has never been so great. We have reached heights where the brain swims, and thoughts are confused, and it is held to be questionable whether we are to turn backward or to move onward to the land of promise; whether we are to be overwhelmed by the material world which we have so marvellously transformed, or with the aid of the secrets we have learned, are to rise Godward to a purer and fairer life of knowledge, justice, and love.

Is the material progress of the nineteenth century a cradle or a grave? Are we to continue to dig and delve and peer into matter until God and the soul fade from our view and we become like the things we work in? To put such questions to the multitude were idle. There is here no affair of votes and majorities. Human nature has not changed, and now, as in the past, crowds follow leaders. What the best minds and the most energetic characters believe and teach and put in practice, the millions will come to accept. The doubt is whether the leaders will be worthy,—the real permanent leaders, for the noisy apparent leaders can never be so. And here we touch the core of the problem which Americans have to solve. No other people has such numbers who are ready to thrust themselves forward as leaders, no other has so few who are really able to lead. In mitigation of this fact, it may be said with truth, that nowhere else is it so difficult to lead; for nowhere else does force rule so little. Every one has opinions; the whole nation is awakened; thousands are able to discuss any subject with plausibility; and to be simply keen-witted and versatile is to be of the crowd. We need men whose intellectual view embraces the history of the race, who are familiar with all literature, who have studied all social movements, who are acquainted with the development of philosophic thought, who are not blinded by physical miracles and industrial wonders, but know how to appreciate all truth, all beauty, all goodness. And to this wide culture they must join the earnestness, the confidence, the charity, and the purity of motive which Christian faith inspires. We need scholars who are saints, and saints who are scholars. We need men of genius who live for God and their country; men of action who seek for light in the company of those who know; men of religion who understand that God reveals himself in science, and works in Nature as in the soul of man, for the good of those who love him. Let us know the right moment, and let us know that it comes for those alone who are prepared.

Chapter II.

Exercise of Mind.

O heavens! how awful is the might of souls
And what they do within themselves while yet
The yoke of earth is new to them, the world
Nothing but a wild field where they were sown.

WORDSWORTH.

Learning is acquaintance with what others have felt, thought, and done; knowledge is the result of what we ourselves have felt, thought, and done. Hence a man knows best what he has taught himself; what personal contact with God, with man, and with Nature has made his own. The important thing, then, is not so much to know the thoughts and loves of others, as to be able ourselves to think truly, and to love nobly. The aim should be to rouse, strengthen, and illumine the mind rather than to store it with learning; and the great educational problem has been, and is, how to give to the soul purity of intention, to the conscience steadfastness, and to the mind force, pliability, and openness to light; or in other words, how to bring philosophy and religion to the aid of the will so that the better self shall prevail and each generation introduce its successor to a higher plane of life.

To this end the efforts of all teachers have, with more or less consciousness, tended; and in this direction too, along winding ways and with periods of arrest or partial return, the race of man has for ages been moving; and he who aspires to gain a place in the van of the mighty army on its heavenward march,—

"And draw new furrows 'neath the healthy morn
And plant the great Hereafter in this Now,"—

may be rash, but his spirit is not ignoble. To him it may not be given "to fan and winnow from the coming step of Time the chaff of custom;" but if he persevere he may confidently hope that his thought and love shall at length rise to fairer and more enduring worlds. He weds himself to things of light, seeks aids to true life within, learns to live with the noble dead, and with the great souls of the present who have uttered the truth whereby they live, in a way more intimate and higher than that granted to those who are with them day by day; for minds are not separated by time and space, but by quality of thought. But to be able to love this life, and with all one's heart to seek this close communion with God, with noble souls, and with Nature is not easy, and it may be that it is impossible for those who are not drawn to it by irresistible instincts. For the intellect, at least, attractions are proportional to destiny; and the art of intellectual life is not most surely learned by those whom circumstances favor, but by those whom will impels onward to exercise of mind; whom neither daily wants, nor animal appetites, nor hope of gain, nor low ambition, nor sneers of worldlings, nor prayers of friends, nor aught else can turn from the pursuit of wisdom; who, with ceaseless labor and with patient thought, eat their way in silence, like caterpillars, to the light, become their own companions, walk uplifted by their own thoughts, and by slow and imperceptible processes are transformed and grow to be the embodiment of the truth and beauty which they see and love.

The overmastering love of mental exercise, of the good of the intellect, is probably never found in formal and prosaic minds; or if so, its first awakening is in the early years when to think is to feel, when the soul, fresh from God, comes trailing clouds of glory, and the sun and moon and stars, and the hills and flowing waters seem but made to crown with joy hearts that love. It is in these dewy dawns that the image of beauty is imprinted on the soul and the sense of mystery awakens. We move about and become a part of all we see, grow akin to stones and leaves and birds, and to all young and happy things. We lose ourselves in life which is poured round us like an unending sea; are natural, healthful, alive to all we see and touch; have no misgivings, but walk as though the eternal God held us by the hand. These are the fair spring days when we suck honey that shall nourish us in the winters of which we do not dream; when sunsets interfuse themselves with all our being until we are dyed in the many-tinted glory; when the miracle of the changing year is the soul's fair seed-time; when lying in the grass, the head resting in clasped hands, while soft white clouds float lazily through azure skies, and the birds warble, and the waters murmur, and the flowers breathe fragrance, we feel a kind of unconscious consciousness of a universal life in Nature. The very rocks seem to be listening to what the leaves whisper; and through the silent eternities we almost see the dead becoming the living, the living the dead, until both grow to be one, and whatever is, is life.

He who has never had these visions; has never heard these airy voices; has never seemed about to catch a glimpse of the inner heart of being, pulsing beneath the veil of visible things; has never felt that he himself is a spirit looking blindly on a universe, which if his eyes could but see and his ears hear, would be revealed as the very heaven of the infinite God,—must forever lack something of the freshness, of the eager delight, with which a poetic mind contemplates the world and follows whither the divine intimations point. This early intercourse with Nature nourishes the soul, deepens the intellect, exalts the imagination, and fills the memory with fair and noble forms and images which abide with us, and as years pass on, gain in softness and purity what they may lose in distinctness of outline and color. This is the source of intellectual wealth, of tranquil moods, of patience in the midst of opposition, of confidence in the fruitfulness of labor and the transforming power of time. Here is given the material which must be moulded into form; the rude blocks which must be cut and dressed and fitted together until they become a spiritual temple wherein the soul may rest at one with God and Nature, and with its own thought and love. To run, to jump, to ride, to swim, to skate, to sit in the shade of trees by flowing water, to watch reapers at their work, to look on orchards blossoming, to dream in the silence that lies amid the hills, to feel the solemn loneliness of deep woods, to follow cattle as they crop the sweet-scented clover,—to learn to know, as one knows a mother's face, every change that comes over the heavens from the dewy freshness of early dawn to the restful calm of evening, from the overpowering mystery of the starlit sky to the tender human look with which the moon smiles upon the earth,—all this is education of a higher and altogether more real kind than it is possible to receive within the walls of a school; and lacking this, nothing shall have power to develop the faculties of the soul in symmetry and completeness. Hence a philosopher has said there are ten thousand chances to one that genius, talent, and virtue shall issue from a farmhouse rather than from a palace. The daily intercourse with Nature in childhood and youth intertwines with noble and enduring objects the passions which form the mind and heart of man, whereas those who are shut out from such communion are necessarily thrown into contact with what is mean and vulgar; and since our early years, whatever our surroundings may have been, seem to us sweet and fair because life itself is then a clear-flowing fountain, they cannot help blending the memory of that innocent and happy time with thoughts of base and mechanical objects, or, it may be, of low and ignoble associates.

He is fortunate who, during the first ten years of his life, escapes the confinement and repression of school, and lives at home in the country amid the fields and the woods, day by day growing familiar with the look on Nature's face, with all her moods, with every common object, with living things in the air and the water and on the earth; who sees the corn sprout, and watches it grow week after week until the yellow harvest waves in the sunlight; who looks with unawed eye on rising thunder-clouds and shouts with glee amid the lightning's play; who learns to know that whatever he looks upon is thereby humanized, and to feel that he is part of all he sees and loves. He will carry with him to the study of the intellectual and spiritual world of men's thoughts shut up in books, a strength of mind, a depth and freshness of heart which only those can own who have drunk at Nature's deep flowing fountain, and come up to life's training-course wet with her dews and with the fragrance of her flowers on their breath. In the eyes of the old Greeks, who first made education a science, the scholar was an idler,—one who had leisure to look about him, to stroll amid the olive groves, to let his eye rest upon the purple hills or the blue sea studded with green isles, to listen to the brooks and the nightingales, to read the lesson the fair earth teaches more than that imprinted on parchment; and the school must still preserve something of this freedom from constraint, must encourage the play of body and of mind, the delight natural to the young in the exercise of strength of whatever kind, and thus as far as possible lighten the labor and drudgery of elementary studies with thoughts of liberty, of beauty, and of excellence. Let the boy feel how good it is to be alive though life meant only the narrow world and the mere surfaces of things with which alone it is possible for him to be acquainted; and then when we ask him to believe that in high thinking and in noble acting he will find a life infinitely more worthy, his eager soul will be inflamed with a desire for knowledge and virtue, and bearing in his heart the strength and wealth of imagination gained from his early experience, his thoughts will turn to great and good men. Dim visions of mighty conquerors, of poets at whose song the woods and waves grow calm, of orators whose words with storm-like force, whatever way they take, sweep with them the wills of men,—will rise before his mind. His young fancy will endow them with preternatural qualities; and he will yearn to draw near, to mingle with them and to catch the secret of their divine power. The germ of the godlike within his bosom bursts and springs. What they were, why may not he also become? What bars are thrown athwart his path, what obstacles hem his way, which, whoever in any age has excelled, has not had to break down and surmount? Here the wise teacher comes to cheer him, to tell him his faith is not wrong, his hope not without promise of attainment if he but trust himself, and bend his whole mind to the task; that whatever goal within the scope of human power, the will sets to itself, it may reach.

In order to develop, strengthen, and confirm this high mood, this noble temper, let him by all means be made acquainted with the language and genius of Greece. Here he will be introduced to a world of thought and sentiment almost as fresh, as fair and many-sided as Nature herself,—the fragrant blossoming in myriad hues and forms of the life and mind of the most richly endowed portion of the human race. Not only are the Greeks the most highly-gifted of all people, but in this classical age they have also this special charm and power,—that the keenest intellectual faculties are in them united with the feelings, hopes, and fancies of a noble and great-hearted youth. Even Socrates and Plato talk like high-souled boys who can see the world only in the light of ideals, for whom what the mind beholds and the heart loves is alone real. How healthfully they look on life, with what delight they breathe the air! What fine contempt have they not of death, thinking no fortune so good as that which comes to the hero who dies in a worthy cause! There is Athens, already the world's university; but no books, no libraries, no lecture-halls, only great teachers who walk about followed by a crowd of youths eager to drink in their words. Here is the Acropolis, with its snow-white temples and propylæum, fair and chaste as though they had been built in heaven and gently lowered to this Attic mound by the hands of angels. There in the Parthenon are the sculptures of Phidias, and yonder in the temple of the Dioscuri, the paintings of Polygnotus,—ideal beauty bodied forth to lure the souls of men to unseen and eternal worlds. If they turn to the east, the isles of the Ægean look up to them like virgins who welcome happy lovers; to the west, Mount Pentelicus, from whose heart the architectural glory of the city has been carved, bids them think what patience will enable man's genius to accomplish; and to the north, Hymettus, fragrant with the breath of a thousand herbs and musical with the hum of bees, stoops with gentle undulations to their feet. They live in the air; their temples are open to the sunlight; their theatres are uncovered to the heavens; and whithersoever they move, they are surrounded by what is fair, noble, and inspiring. This free and happy life in the company of great teachers becomes the stimulus to the keenest exercise of mind. They are as eager to see things in a true light as they are quick to sympathize with whatever is heroic or beautiful; and all their talk is of truth and justice, the good, the fair, the excellent, of philosophy, religion, poetry, and art, and of whatever else seems favorable to human life and to the development of ideal manhood. Of the merely useful they have the scorn of young and inexperienced minds; and Hippocrates proclaims himself ready to give Protagoras, not only whatever he himself possesses, but also the property of his friends, if he will but teach him wisdom. Superior knowledge was to them of all things the most admirable and the most to be desired. What noble thoughts have they not concerning education? "An intelligent man," says Plato, "will prize those studies which result in his soul getting soberness, righteousness, and wisdom, and will less value the others." The culture of the mind is made a kind of religion, in the spreading of which the personal influence of the teacher is not less active than the truths he sets forth. Bonds of affection bind the disciple to the master whose words have for him the sacredness of wisdom and the charm of genius, power to confirm the will, and warmth and color whereby the imagination is raised.

This secret of making knowledge attractive, of clothing truth in chaste and beautiful language, of associating it with whatever is fair and noble in Nature, and of relating it to life and conduct, which is part of the genius of Greece, still lives in her literature; and to read the words of her poets, orators, and philosophers is to feel the presence of a high and active spirit, is to breathe in an intellectual atmosphere of light and liberty, is of itself enlargement and cultivation of mind. Hence, in the realms of thought, the Greeks are the civilizers and emancipators of the world; and whoever thinks, is to some extent their debtor. The music of their eloquence and poetry can never grow silent; the forms of beauty their genius has created can never perish, and never cease to win the admiration and love of noble minds and gentle hearts, or to be the inspiration, generation after generation, to high thoughts and heroic moods. So long as glory, beauty, freedom, light, and gladness shall seem good and fair, so long will the finer spirits of the world feel the attraction and the charm of Greece, and know the sweet surprise which thrilled the heart of Keats when first he read Homer:—

"Then felt I like some watcher of the skies
When a new planet swims into his ken,
Or like stout Cortez when with eagle eyes
He stared at the Pacific, and all his men
Looked at each other with a wild surmise,
Silent, upon a peak in Darien."

In a less degree, Roman literature, which is the offspring of Greek culture, has value as an intellectual stimulus and discipline. Here also the youthful mind is brought into the presence of a great and noble people, who, if they have less genius and a duller sense of beauty than the Greeks, excel them in steadiness of purpose, in dignity of character, in reverence for law and religion, and above all in the art of governing.

The educational value of the classics does not lie so much in the Greek and Latin languages as in the type of mind, the sense of proportion and beauty, the heroic temper, the philosophic mood, the keen relish for high enterprise, and the joyful love of life which they make known to us. The world to which they introduce us is so remote that the pre-occupations and vulgarities of the present, by which we all are hemmed and warped, fall away from us; and it is at the same time so real and of such absorbing interest that we are caught up in spirit and carried to the Attic Plain and the hills of Latium. They are useful, not because they teach us anything that may not be learned and learned more accurately from modern books, but because they move the mind, fire the heart, ennoble and refine the imagination in a way which nothing else has power to do. They are sources of inspiration; they first roused the modern mind to activity; and the potency of their influence can never cease to be felt by those whose aptitudes lead them to the love of intellectual perfection, who delight in the free play of the mind, who are attracted by what is symmetrical, who have the instinct for beauty, who swim in a current of ideas as naturally as birds fly in the air. They appeal to the mind as a whole, stimulate all its faculties, awaken a many-sided sympathy both with Nature and with the world of men. They widen our view of life, bring forth in us the consciousness of our kinship with the human race, and of the application to ourselves, however common and uninspiring our surroundings may be, of the best thoughts and noblest deeds which have ever sprung from the brain and heart of man. They help to make one, again to quote Plato, "A lover, not of a part of wisdom, but of the whole; who has a taste for every sort of knowledge, and is curious to learn and is never satisfied; who has magnificence of mind, and is a spectator of all time and all existence; who is harmoniously constituted, of a well-proportioned and gracious mind, whose own nature will move spontaneously toward the true being of everything; who has a good memory, and is quick to learn, noble, gracious, the friend of truth, justice, courage, temperance." The ideal presented is that of complete harmonious culture, the aim of which is not to make an artisan, a physician, a merchant, a lawyer, but a man alive in all his faculties, touching the world at many points, for whom all knowledge is desirable, all beauty lovable, and for whom fine bearing and noble acting are indispensable.

It is needless to point out in what, or why, the Greeks failed, since here there is question only of intellectual life, and in this they did not fail. Nor is there any thought, in what has here been said, of depreciating the worth of the study of science, without a certain knowledge of which no one, in this age, can in any true sense, be called educated. Whoever, indeed, learns a language properly, acquires scientific knowledge; and the Greeks are not only the masters in poetry and eloquence, they are also the guides to the right use of reason and to scientific method, and the teachers of mathematics, logic, and physics. He who pursues culture, in the Greek spirit, who desires to see things as they are, to know the best that has been thought and done by men, will fear nothing so much as the exclusion of any truth, and he will be anxious to acquaint himself not only with the method, but as far as possible with the facts, of physical science. Still he perceives that however great the value of natural knowledge may be, it is, as an instrument of culture, inferior to literature. We are educated by what calls forth in us love and admiration, by what creates the exalted mood and the steadfast purpose. In bowing with reverence to what is above us, we are uplifted. When we are moved, we are more alive; we are stronger, tenderer, nobler. Now to look upon Nature with the detective eye of the man of science is to be cold and unsympathetic; to learn by methodic experiment is to gain knowledge, which, since it is only remotely or indirectly related to life, is but little interesting. Such knowledge is a fragment, and a fragment extremely difficult to fit into the temple built by thought and love, by hope and imagination; and hence when we have learned a great deal about chemical elements, geologic epochs, correlation of forces, and sidereal spaces, we are rather astonished than enlightened. We are brought into the presence of a world which is not that of the senses, nor yet that which faith, hope, and love forebode; and the bearing it may have upon human life is of more interest to us than the facts made known. We are, indeed, curious to know whatever may, with any certainty, be told us of atoms and biogenesis; but our real concern is to learn what significance such truth may have in its relation to questions of God and the soul.

There is doubtless a disciplinary value in the study of physical science. It trains the mind to habits of patient attention, of careful observation, teaches the danger of hasty generalization, and diminishes intellectual conceit; but these results may also be obtained by other means. The aim of education is not simply to develop this or the other faculty, however indispensable, nor yet to make one thoroughly conversant with a particular order of facts, but the aim is to bring about a conscious participation in the life of the race, to evoke all the powers of man, so that his whole being shall be quickened and made responsive to the touch of things seen and unseen; and the study of science is less adapted to the attainment of this end than the study of human letters. The scientific temper draws to specialties; and specialists are narrow, are incomplete. They, each in his own line, do good work, and are the chief agents for the increase of natural knowledge, and are, we may grant, leaders in every kind of improvement; but like the operatives who provide our comforts and luxuries, they are themselves warped and crippled by what they do. The habit of looking at a single order of facts, coldly and always from the same point of view, takes from the mind flexibility, weakens the imagination, and puts fetters on the soul; and hence though it is important that there be specialists, the kind of education by which they are formed, while it is suited to make a geologist, a chemist, a mathematician, or a botanist, is not suited to call forth the free and harmonious play of all man's powers. We do not live on facts alone, much less on facts of a single kind. Religion and poetry, love, hope, and imagination are as essential to our well-being as science. Human life is knowledge, is faith, is conduct, is beauty, is manners; it unfolds itself in many directions and shoots its roots into infinitude; and for the general purposes of education, science is learned to best advantage when it is embodied in literature, and its methods and results, rather than the details of its work, are presented to us. Whatever it is able to do, to improve the mind, to widen the range of thought, to give true notions of the workings of Nature,—it will do for whoever learns accurately its general conceptions and results; and these cannot remain unknown to him whose aim is culture, for such an one is, as Plato says, "A lover not of a part of wisdom, but of the whole, and has a taste for every sort of knowledge, and is curious to learn, and is never satisfied; and though he will not know medicine like a physician, or the heavens like an astronomer, or the vegetable kingdom like a botanist, his mind will play over all these realms with freedom, and he will know how to relate the principles and facts of all the sciences to our sense for beauty, for conduct, for life and religion in a way which a mere specialist can never find." And his view will not only be wider and less impeded, it will also be deeper than that of the man of science; for he who sees but one order of things sees only their surfaces, just as he who sees but one thing sees nothing at all.

It would be a mistake to imagine that the ideal here commended, means superficial accomplishments, an excessive love of style and the ornaments of poetry and eloquence, or preoccupation in favor of aught external or frivolous. It is the very opposite of dilettanteism, and if it mean anything, means thoroughness, and a thoroughness which can come only of untiring labor carried on through many years; for time and intercourse with men and varied experience are indispensable elements. It is like the ideal of religion which makes the saint think himself a sinner; it is as exacting as the miser's thought which makes millions seem to be beggary; like the artist's vision, like the poet's dream, it allures and yet forbids hope of attainment. The seeker after wisdom must have a high purpose, a strong soul, and the purest love of truth. He cannot live in the senses alone, nor in the mind, nor in the heart alone, but the spiritual being, which is himself, yearns for whatever is good, whatever is true, whatever is fair, and so he finds himself akin to the infinite God and to all that he has made. When his thought is carried out to atoms weaving the garment which is our body, and moulding the world we see and touch; when he beholds motion lighting, warming, thrilling the universe,—he is filled with intellectual joy, but at the same time he perceives that all this is but a phase of truth; that God and the boundless facts are infinitely more than drilled atomics marshalled rank on rank until they form the countless hosts of the heavens. When the men of science have labelled the elements, and put tickets upon all natural compounds, and with complacency declare that this is the whole truth, he looks on the flowers around him and the blooming children, on the stars above his head, on the sun slow wheeling down the western horizon, on the moon climbing some eastern hill, and his inmost soul is glad because he feels the thrill of the infinite, living Spirit, and forebodes to what fair countries we are bound.

And when they proclaim the wonders science has wrought,—increase of physical enjoyment and social comfort; the yoking of lightning and steam to make them work for man; the providing of more abundant food; the building of more wholesome dwellings; the lengthening of life; temporal benefits of every kind,—he joins with those who utter praise, but knows that infinitely more than all this goes to the making of man's life. So he turns his mind in many directions, and while he looks on the truth in science, does not grow blind to the truth in religion; while he knows the value of what is practically useful, understands also the priceless worth of what is noble and beautiful, and his acquaintance with many kinds of thought, with many shades of opinion confirms him, as Joubert says, in the acceptance of the best.

Chapter III.

The Love of Excellence.

> Why is this glorious creature to be found
> One only in ten thousand? what one is,
> Why may not millions be? what bars are thrown
> By Nature in the way of such a hope?
>
> WORDSWORTH.

He teaches to good purpose who inspires the love of excellence, and who sends his pupils forth from the school's narrow walls with such desire for self-improvement that the whole world becomes to them a God-appointed university. And why shall not every youth hope to enter the narrow circle of those for whom to live, is to think, who behold "the bright countenance of truth in the quiet and still air of delightful studies." An enlightened mind is like a fair and pleasant friend who comes to cheer us in every hour of loneliness and gloom; it is like noble birth which admits to all best company; it is like wealth which surrounds us with whatever is rarest and most precious; it is like virtue which lives in an atmosphere of light and serenity, and is itself enough for itself. Whatever our labors, our cares, our disappointments, a free and open mind, by holding us in communion with the highest and the fairest, will fill the soul with strength and joy. The artist, day by day, year in and year out, hangs over his work, and finds enough delight in the beauty he creates; and shall not the friend of the soul be glad in striving ceaselessly to make his knowledge and his love less unlike the knowledge and the love of God? Seldom is opportunity of victory offered to great captains, the orator rarely finds fit theme and audience, hardly shall the hero meet with occasions worthy of the sacrifice of life; but he who labors to shape his mind to the heavenly forms of truth and beauty beholds them ever present and appealing. Life without thought and love is worthless; and to the best men and women belong only those who cultivate with earnestness and perseverance their spiritual faculties, who strive daily to know more, to love more, to be more beautiful. They are the chosen ones, and all others, even though they sit on thrones, are but the crowd.

Without a free and open mind there is no high and glad human life. You may as well point to the savage drowsing in his tent, or to cattle knee-deep in clover, and bid me think them high, as to ask me to admire where I can behold neither intelligence nor love. All that we possess is qualified by what we are. Gold makes not the miser rich, nor its lack a true man poor; and he who has gained insight into the fair truth that he is a part of all he sees and loves, is richer than kings, and lives like a god in his universe. Possibilities for us are measured by the kind of work in which we put our hearts. If a man's thoughts are wholly busy with carpentering do not expect him to become anything else than a carpenter; but if his aim is to build up his own being, to make his mind luminous, his heart tender and pure, his will steadfast, who but God shall fix a limit beyond which he may not hope to go. Education, indeed, cannot confer organic power; but it alone gives us the faculty to perceive how infinitely wonderful and fair are man's endowments, how boundless his inheritance, how full of deathless hope is that to which he may aspire. Religion, philosophy, poetry, science,—all bring us into the presence of an ideal of ceaseless growth toward an all-perfect Infinite, dimly discerned and unapproachable, but which fascinates the soul and haunts the imagination with its deep mystery, until what we long for becomes more real than all that we possess, and yearning is our highest happiness. Ah! who would throw a veil over the vision on which young eyes rest when young hearts feel that ideal things alone are real? Who would rob them of this divine principle of progress which makes growth the best of life?

"Many are our joys
In youth; but oh, what happiness to live
When every hour brings palpable access
Of knowledge, when all knowledge is delight!"

In all ages, we know those made wise by experience, which teaches us to expect little, whether of ourselves or others, have made the thoughts and hopes of youth a jest, even as men have made religion a jest, having nothing to offer us in compensation for its loss, but witticisms and despair.

This is the fatal fault of life, that when we have obtained what is good,—as wealth, position, wife, and friends,—we lose all hope of the best, and with our mockery discourage those who have ideal aims; who, remembering how the soul felt in life's dawn, retain a sense of God's presence in the world, to whom with growing faculties they aspire, feeling that whatsoever point they reach, they still have something to pursue. This is the principle of the diviner mind in all high and heroic natures; this is the spring-head of deeds that make laws, of "thoughts that enrich the blood of the world;" this is the power which gives to resolve the force of destiny, and clothes the soul with the heavenliest strength and beauty when it stands single and alone, of men abandoned and almost of God.

There is little danger that too many shall ever hearken to the invitation from the fair worlds to which all souls belong, and where alone they can be luminous and free. For centuries, now, what innumerable voices have pleaded with men to make themselves worthy of heaven; while they have moved on heedless of the heaven that lies about us here, placing their hopes and aims in material and perishable elements, athirst neither for truth, nor beauty, nor aught that is divinely good! They sleep, they wake, they eat, they drink; they tread the beaten path with ceaseless iteration, and so they die. If one come appealing for culture of intellect, not because they who know, are stronger than the ignorant and make them their servants, but because an open, free, and flexible mind is good and fair, better than birth, position, and wealth, they turn away as though he trifled with their common-sense. Life, they say, is not for knowledge, but knowledge for life; and they neither truly know, nor live. And if here and there some nobler soul stand forth, he degrades himself to an aspirant to fame, forgetting truth and love.

Enough there are on earth who reap and sow,
Enough who give their lives to common gain,
Enough who toil with spade and axe and plane,
Enough who sail the seas where rude winds blow;
Enough who make their life unmeaning show,
Enough who plead in courts, who physic pain;
Enough who follow in the lover's train,
And taste of wedded hearts the bliss and woe.

A few at least may love the poet's song,
May walk with him, their visionary guide,
Far from the crowd, nor do the world a wrong;

Or on his wings through deep blue skies may glide
And float, by light transfused, like clouds along
Above the earth and over oceans wide.

With unresting, wearing thought and labor we are striving to make earth more habitable. We drag forth from its inner parts whatever treasures are hidden there; with steam's mighty force we mould brute matter into every fair and serviceable form; we build great cities, we spread the fabric of our trade; the engine's iron heart goes throbbing through tunnelled mountains and over storm-swept seas to bear us and our wealth to all regions of the globe; we talk to one another from city to city, and from continent to continent along ocean's oozy depths the lightning flashes our words, spreading beneath our eyes each morning the whole world's gossip,—but in the midst of this miraculous transformation, we ourselves remain small, hard, and narrow, without great thoughts or great loves or immortal hopes. We are a crowd where the highest and the best lose individuality, and are swept along as though democracy were a tyranny of the average man under which superiority of whatever kind is criminal. Our population increases, our cities grow, our roads are lengthened, our machinery is made more perfect, the number of our schools is multiplied, our newspapers are read in ever-widening circles, the spirit of humanity and of freedom breathes through our life; but the individual remains common-place and uninteresting. He lacks intelligence, has no perception of what is excellent, no faith in ideals, no reverence for genius, no belief in any highest sort of man who has not shown his worth in winning wealth, position, or notoriety. We have a thousand poets and no poetry, a thousand orators and no eloquence, a thousand philosophers and no philosophy. Every city points to its successful men who have millions, but are themselves poor and unintelligent; to its writers who, having sold their talent to newspapers and magazines, sink to the level of those they address, dealing only with what is of momentary interest, or if the question be deep, they move on the surface, lest the many-eyed crowd lose sight of them. The preacher gets an audience and pay on condition that he stoop to the gossip which centres around new theories, startling events, and mechanical schemes for the improvement of the country. If to get money be the end of writing and preaching, then must we seek to please the multitude who are willing to pay those who entertain and amuse them. Will not our friends, even, conceive a mean opinion of our ability, if we fail to gain public recognition?

So we make ourselves "motleys to the view, and sell cheap what is most dear." We must, perforce, show the endowment which can be brought to perfection only if it be permitted to grow in secrecy and solitude. The worst foe of excellence is the desire to appear; for when once we have made men talk of us, we seem to be doing nothing if they are silent, and thus the love of notoriety becomes the bane of true work and right living. To be one of a crowd is not to be at all; and if we are resolved to put our thoughts and acts to the test of reason, and to live for what is permanently true and great, we must consent, like the best of all ages, to be lonely in the world. All life, except the life of thought and love, is dull and superficial. The young love for a while, and are happy; a few think; and for the rest existence is but the treadmill of monotonous sensation. There are but few, who, through work and knowledge, through faith and hope and love, seek to escape from the narrowness and misery of life to the summits of thought where the soul breathes a purer air, and whence is seen the fairer world the multitude forebodes. There are but few whose life is

> "Effort and expectation and desire,
> And something evermore about to be;"

but few who understand how much the destiny of Man hangs upon single persons; but few who feel that what they love and teach, millions must know and love.

> "A people is but the attempt of many
> To rise to the completer life of one;
> And those who live as models for the mass
> Are singly of more value than them all."

Only the noblest souls awaken within us divine aspirations. They are the music, the poetry, which warms and illumines whole generations; they are the few who, born with rich endowments, by ceaseless labor develop their powers until they become capable of work which, were it not for them, could not be done at all. History is the biography of aristocrats, of the chosen ones with whom all improvement originates, who found States, establish civilizations, create literatures, and teach wisdom. They work not for themselves; for in spite of human selfishness and the personal aims of the ambitious, the poet, the scholar, and the statesman bless the world. They lead us through happy isles; they clothe our thoughts and hopes with beauty and with strength; they dissipate the general gloom; they widen the sphere of life; they bring the multitude beneath the sway of law.

Now, here in America, once for all, whatever the thoughtless may imagine, we have lost faith in the worth of artificial distinctions. Indeed plausible arguments may be found to prove that the kind of man democracy tends to form, has no reverence for distinctions of whatever kind, and is without ideals, and that as he is envious of men made by money, so he looks with the contempt of unenlightened common-sense upon those whom character and intellect raise above him. This is not truth. The higher you lift the mass, the more will they acknowledge and appreciate worth, the clearer will they see that what makes man human, beautiful, and beneficent is conduct and intelligence; and so increasing enlightenment will turn thought and admiration from position and wealth, from the pomp and show of life to what makes a man's self, his character, his mind, his manners even,—for the source of manners lies within us. In a society like ours, the chosen ones, the best, the models of life, and the leaders of thought will be distinguished from the crowd not by accident or circumstance, but by inner strength and beauty, by finer knowledge, by purer love, by a deeper faith in God, by a more steadfast trust that it must, and shall be, well with a world which God makes and rules, and which to the fairest mind is fairest, and to the holiest soul most sacred.

Here and now, if ever anywhere at any time, there is need of men, there is appeal to what is godlike in man, calling upon us to rise above our prosperities, our politics, our mechanical aims and implements, and to turn the courage, energy, and practical sense which have wrought with miraculous power in developing the material resources of America, to the cultivation of our spiritual faculties. We alone of the great modern nations are without classical writers of our own, without a national literature. The thought and love of this people, its philosophy, poetry, and art lies yet in the bud; and our tens of thousands of books, even the better sort, must perish to enrich the soil that nourishes a life of heavenly promise. Hitherto we have been sad imitators of the English, but not the best the English have done will satisfy America. Their language indeed will remain ours, and their men of genius, above all their poets, will enrich our minds with great thoughts nobly expressed. But a literature is a national growth; it is the expression of a people's life and character, the more or less perfect utterance of what it loves, aims at, believes in, hopes for; it has the qualities and the defects of the national spirit; it bears the marks of the thousand influences that help to make that spirit what it is,—and English literature cannot be American literature, for the simple reason that Americans are not Englishmen, any more than they are Germans or Frenchmen. We must be ourselves in our thinking and writing, as in our living, or be insignificant, for it is a man's life that gives meaning to his thought; and to write as a disciple is to write in an inferior way, since the mind at its best is illumined by truth itself and not taught by the words of another. It is not to be believed that this great, intelligent, yearning American world will content itself with the trick and mannerism of foreign accent and style, or that those who build on any other than the broad foundation of our own national life shall be accepted as teachers and guides. There is, of course, no method known to man by which a great author may be formed; no science which teaches how a literature may be created. The men who have written what the world will not permit to die have written generally without any clear knowledge of the worth of their work, just as great discoverers and inventors seem to stumble on what they seek; nevertheless one may hope by right endeavor to make himself capable of uttering true thoughts so that they shall become intelligible and attractive to others; he may educate himself to know and love the best that has been spoken and written by men of genius, and so become a power to lift the aims and enlarge the views of his fellow-men. If many strive in this way to unfold their gifts and to cultivate their faculties, their influence will finally pervade the life and thought of thousands, and it may be of the whole people.

I do not at all forget Aristotle's saying that "life is practice and not theory;" that men are born to do and suffer, and not to dream and weave systems; that conduct and not culture is the basis of character and the source of strength; that a knowledge of Nature is of vastly more importance to our material comfort and progress than philosophy, poetry, and art. This is not to be called in question; but in this country and age it seems hardly necessary that it be emphasized, for what is the whole world insisting upon but the necessity of scientific instruction, the importance of practical education, the cultivation of the money-getting faculty and habit, and the futility of philosophy, poetry, and art? Who is there that denies the worth of what is useful? Where is there one who does not approve and encourage whatever brings increase of wealth? Are we not all ready to applaud projects which give promise of providing more abundant food, better clothing, and more healthful surrounding for the poor? Does not our national genius seem to lie altogether in the line of what is practically useful? Is it not our boast and our great achievement that we have in a single century made the wilderness of a vast continent habitable, have so ploughed and drained and planted and built that it can now easily maintain hundreds of millions in gluttonous plenty? Is not our whole social and political organization of a kind which fits us to deal with questions and affairs that concern our temporal and material welfare? What innumerable individuals among us are congressmen, legislators, supervisors, bank and school directors, presidents of boards and companies, committee-men, councilmen, heads of lodges and societies, lawyers, professors, teachers, editors, colonels, generals, judges, party-leaders, so that the sovereign people seems to have life and being only in its titled representatives! What does this universal reign of title and office mean but the practical education which responsibility gives? If from the midst of this paradise of utility, materialism, and business, a voice is raised to plead for culture, for intelligence, for beauty, for philosophy, poetry, and art, why need any one take alarm? While human nature remains what it is, can there be danger that the many will be drawn away from what appeals to the senses, to what the soul loves and yearns for? If the Almighty God does not win the multitude to the love of righteousness and wisdom, how shall the words of man prevail?

It is a mistake to oppose use to beauty, the serviceable to the excellent, since they belong together. Beauty is the blossom that makes the fruit-tree fair and fragrant. Life means more than meat and drink, house and clothing. To live is also to admire, to love, to lose one's self in the contemplation of the splendor with which Nature is clothed. Human life is the marriage of souls with things of light. Its basis, aim, and end is love, and love makes its object beautiful. Man may not even consent to eat, except with decency and grace; he must have light and flowers and the rippling music of kindly speech, that as far as possible he may forget that his act is merely animal and useful. He will lose sight of the fact that clothing is intended for protection and comfort, rather than not dress to make himself beautiful. To speak merely to be understood, and not to speak also with ease and elegance, is not to be a gentleman. How easily words find the way to the heart when uttered in melodious cadence by the lips of the fair and young. Home is the centre and seat of whatever is most useful to us; and yet to think of home is to think of spring-time and flowers, of the songs of birds and flowing waters, of the voices of children, of floating clouds and sunsets that linger as though heaven were loath to bid adieu to earth. The warmth, the color, and the light of their boyish days still glow in the hearts and imagination of noble men, and redeem the busy trafficking world of their daily life from utter vulgarity. What hues has not God painted on the air, the water, the fruit, and the grain that are the very substance and nutriment of our bodies? Beauty is nobly useful. It illumines the mind, raises the imagination, and warms the heart. It is not an added quality, but grows from the inner nature of things; it is the thought of God working outward. Only from drunken eyes can you with paint and tinsel hide inward deformity. The beauty of hills and waves, of flowers and clouds, of children at play, of reapers at work, of heroes in battle, of poets inspired, of saints rapt in adoration,—rises from central depths of being, and is concealed from frivolous minds. Even in the presence of death, the hallowing spirit of beauty is felt. The full-ripe fruit that gently falls in the quiet air of long summer days, the yellow sheaves glinting in the rays of autumn's sun, the leaf which the kiss of the hoar frost has made blood-red and loosened from the parent stem,—are images of death but they suggest only calm and pleasant thoughts. The Bedouin, who, sitting amid the ruins of Ephesus, thinks but of his goats and pigs, heedless of Diana's temple, Alexander's glory, and the words of Saint Paul, is the type of those who place the useful above the excellent and the fair; and as men who in their boards of trade buy and sell cattle and corn, dream not of green fields and of grain turning to gold in the sun of June, so we all, in the business and worry of life, lose sight of beauty which makes the heart glad and keeps it young.

The mind of man is the earthly home of beauty, and if any real thing were fair as the tender thought of imaginative youth, heaven were not far. All we love is but our thought of what only thought makes known and makes beautiful, and for what we know love's thought may be the essence of all things.

Fairer than waters where soft moonlight lies,
Than flowers that slumber on the breast of Spring,
Than leafy trees in June when glad birds sing,
Than a cool summer dawn, than sunset skies;

Than love, gleaming through Beauty's deep blue eyes,
Than laughing child, than orchards blossoming;
Than girls whose voices make the woodland ring,
Than ruby lips that utter sweet replies,—

Fairer than these, than all that may be seen,
Is the poetic mind, which sheds the light

Of heaven on earthly things, as Night's young Queen
Forth-looking from some jagged mountain height
Clothes the whole earth with her soft silvery sheen
And makes the beauty whereof eyes have sight.

Nature is neither sad nor joyful. We but see in her the reflection of our own minds. Gay scenes depress the melancholy, and gloomy prospects have not the power to rob the happy of their contentment. The spring may fill us with fresh and fragrant thoughts, or may but remind us of all the hopes and joys we have lost; and autumn will speak to one of decay and death, to another of sleep and rest, after toil, to prepare for a new and brighter awakening. All the glory of dawn and sunset is but etheric waves thrilling the vapory air and impinging on the optic nerve; but behind it all is the magician who sees and knows, who thinks and loves. "It is the mind that makes the body rich." Thoughts take shape and coloring from souls through which they pass; and a free and open mind looks upon the world in the mood in which a fair woman beholds herself in a mirror. The world is his as much as the face is hers. If we could live in the fairest spot of earth, and in the company of those who are dear, the source of our happiness would still be our own thought and love; and if they are great and noble, we cannot be miserable however meanly surrounded. What is reality but a state of soul, finite in man, infinite in God? Theory underlies fact, and to the divine mind all things are godlike and beautiful. The chemical elements are as sweet and pure in the buried corpse as in the blooming body of youth; and it is defective intellect, the warp of ignorance and sin, which hides from human eyes the perfect beauty of the world.

"Earth's crammed with heaven,
And every common bush afire with God;
But only he who sees, takes off his shoes."

What we all need is not so much greater knowledge, as a luminous and symmetrical mind which, whatsoever way it turn, shall reflect the things that are, not in isolation and abstraction, but in the living unity and harmony wherein they have their being.

The worth of religion is infinite, the value of conduct is paramount; but he who lacks intellectual culture, whatever else he may be, is narrow, awkward, unintelligent. The mirror of his soul is dim, the motions of his spirit are sluggish, and the divine image which is himself is blurred.

But let no one imagine that this life of the soul in the mind is easy; for it is only less difficult than the life of the soul in God. To learn many things; to master this or that science; to have skill in law or medicine; to acquaint one's self with the facts of history, with the opinions of philosophers or the teachings of theologians,—is comparatively not a difficult task; and there are hundreds who are learned, who are skillful, who are able, who have acuteness and depth and information, for one who has an open, free, and flexible mind,—which is alive and active in many directions, touching the world of God and Nature at many points, and beholding truth and beauty from many sides; which is serious, sober, and reasonable, but also fresh, gentle, and sympathetic; which enters with equal ease into the philosopher's thought, the poet's vision, and the ecstasy of the saint; which excludes no truth, is indifferent to no beauty, refuses homage to no goodness. The ideal of culture indeed, like that of religion, like that of art, lies beyond our reach, since the truth and beauty which lure us on, and flee the farther the longer we pursue, are nothing less than the eternal and infinite God.

And culture, if it is not to end in mere frivolity and gloss, must be pursued, like religion and art, with earnestness and reverence. If the spirit in which we work is not deep and holy, we may become accomplished but we shall not gain wisdom, power, and love. The beginner seeks to convert his belief into knowledge; but the trained thinker knows that knowledge ends in belief, since beyond our little islets of intellectual vision, lies the boundless, fathomless expanse of unknown worlds where faith and hope alone can be our guides. Once individual man was insignificant; but now the earth itself is become so,—a mere dot in infinite space, where, for a moment, men wriggle like animalcules in a drop of water. And if at times a flash of light suddenly gleam athwart the mind, and it seem as though we were about to get a glimpse into the inner heart of being, the brightness quickly dies, and only the surfaces of things remain visible. Oh, the unimaginable length of ages when on the earth there was no living thing! then life's ugly, slimy beginnings; then the conscious soul's fitful dream stretching forth to endless time and space; then the final sleep in abysmal night with its one star of hope twinkling before the all-hidden throne of God, in the shadow of whose too great light faith kneels and waits!

Why shall he whose mind is free, symmetrical, and open, be tempted to vain glory, to frivolous boasting? Shall not life be more solemn and sacred to him than to another? Shall he indulge scorn for any being whom God has made, for any thought which has strengthened and consoled the human heart? Shall he not perceive, more clearly than others, that the unseen Power by whom all things are, is akin to thought and love, and that they alone bring help to man who make him feel that faith and hope mean good, and are fountains of larger and more enduring life? The highest mind, like the purest heart, is a witness of the soul and of God.

Chapter IV.

Culture and the Spirit of the Age.

> But try, I urge,—the trying shall suffice:
> The aim, if reached or not, makes great the life.
>
> BROWNING.

The mass of mankind, if we pass the whole race in review, are sunk in gross ignorance; and even in civilized nations, where education is free, the multitude have but a rude acquaintance with the elements of knowledge. Their ability to read and write hardly serves intellectual and moral ends; and such learning as they possess seems only to weaken their power to admire and love what is best in life and thought.

If we turn to the more cultivated, whose numbers even in the most enlightened countries are not great, we find but here and there an individual who has anything better than a sort of mechanical cleverness. Students, it has been said, on leaving college, quickly divide into two classes,—those who have learned nothing, and those who have forgotten everything. In the professions, the lawyer tends to become an advocate, the physician an empiric, the theologian a dogmatist; and these are but instances of a general falling away from ideals. The student of physical science is subdued to what he works in; the man of letters loses depth and earnestness; and the teacher, whose business it is to rouse and illumine souls, shrivels until he becomes merely a repeater of facts and doctrines in which there is no life, no power to exalt the imagination or to give tone to the intellect. The teacher cannot create talent, and his best work lies in stimulating and directing energy and impulse; but this he seldom strives to do or to make himself capable of doing; and hence pupils very generally leave school as men quit a prison, with a sense of emancipation, and with a desire to forget both the place and the kind of life there encouraged. A talent is like seed-corn,—it bears within itself the power to break the confining walls and to spring upward to light, if only it be sown in proper soil, where the rain and the sunshine fall; but this is a truth which those who make education a business are slow to accept. They repress; they overawe; they are dictatorial; they prescribe rules and methods for minds which can gain strength and wisdom only by following the bent given by their endowments,—and thus the young, who are most easily discouraged in things which concern their highest gifts, lose heart, turn away from ideals, and abandon the pursuit of excellence. The nobler the mind, the greater the danger of its being wrongly dealt with. We seldom find a man whose thinking has helped to form opinion and to create literature, who, if he care to say what he feels, will not declare that his scholastic training was bad. Milton, Gray, Dryden, Wordsworth, Byron, Cowley, Addison, Gibbon, Locke, Shelley, and Cowper had no love for the schools to which they were sent; Swift and Goldsmith received no college honors; and Pope, Thomson, Burns, and Shakespeare had little or nothing to do with institutions of learning. A man educates himself; and the best work teachers can do, is to inspire the love of mental exercise and a living faith in the power of labor to develop faculty, and to open worlds of use and delight which are infinite, and which each individual must rediscover for himself. It is the educator's business to cherish the aspirations of the young, to inspire them with confidence in themselves, and to make them feel and understand that no labor can be too great or too long, if its result be cultivation and enlightenment of mind. For them ideals are real; their life is as yet wrapped in the bud; and to encourage them to believe that if they are but true to themselves, the flower and the fruit will be fair and health-bringing, is to open for them the fountain of hope and noble endeavor.

What men have done, men can still do. Nay, shall we not rather believe that the best is yet to be done? The peoples whom we call ancient were but rude beginners. We are the true ancients, the inheritors of all the wisdom and all the heroism of the past. We stand in a wider world, and move forward with more conscious purpose along more open ways. Of the past we see but the summits, illumined by the rays of genius and glory. Could we look upon the plains where the multitudes lie in darkness, wearing the triple chain of servitude, ignorance, and want, we should understand how fair and beneficent our own age is. Enthusiasm for the past cannot inspire the best intellectual work. The heart turns to the past; but the mind looks to the future, and is forever untwisting the cords which bind us to the things that pleased a childlike fancy. To grow is to outgrow; and whatever of the past survives, survives, as the very word implies, because it is still living and applicable here and now. Let not the young believe that the age of the heroic and godlike is gone. Good and the means of good are not harder to reconcile to-day than they were a hundred or a thousand years ago, and they who have a heart may now, as the best have done in the past, wring even from despair the courage on which victory loves to smile. If we are weak and inferior the fault lies in ourselves, not in the age. We are the age; and if we but will and work, opportunities are offered us to become and to perform whatever may crown and glorify a human soul. The time for doing best things, like eternity, is ever present. Let but the man stand forth, and he will find and do his work.

We are too near our own age to discern its true glory, which shall best appear from the vantage-ground of another century; but surely we can feel that it throbs with life, with immortal yearnings, with ever-growing desire to give to all men higher thoughts and purer loves. Society, the State, the Church, the individual, are striving with conscious purpose to make life moral and intelligent. We have become more humane than men have ever been, and accept more fully the duty and the task of extending the domain of justice, of goodness, and of truth. The aim of our civilization is not merely to instruct the ignorant, but to make ignorance impossible; not merely to feed the hungry, but to do away with famine; not merely to visit the captive, but to make captivity the means of his regeneration. Already the chains of the slave have been broken, and the earth has become the home of God's free children. Disease has been tracked to its secret hiding-places, and barriers have been built against pestilence and contagion. War has become less frequent and less barbarous; persecution for opinion and belief has become rare; man's inhumanity to woman, which is the deepest stain upon the history of the race, has yielded to the influence of religion and knowledge; and with ever-increasing force the truth is borne in upon those who think and observe, that the fate of the rich and high-placed cannot be separated from that of the poor and lowly. While we earnestly strive to control and repress every kind of moral evil, we feel that society itself is responsible for sin and crime, and that social and political conditions and constitutions must change, until the weak and the heavy-laden are protected from the heartlessness of the strong and fortunate. Not only must those who labor with their hands have larger opportunities than hitherto have ever been given them, but in the whole social life of man there must be more justice, more love, more tenderness, more of the spirit of Christ, than hitherto has ever been found there.

What marvellous, intellectual work are we not doing? What admirable expression of the highest truth do we not find in the best writers of our age! It is not all pure gold; but whether we take a religious, a moral, or an intellectual point of view, we may not affirm of the literature of any age or country that it is perfect. When man clothes in words what he thinks and loves, what he knows and believes, his work bears the marks of his defects not less than those of his qualities. Nay, if we turn to the Bible itself, how much do we not find there which we either fail to comprehend or are unable to apply! Has not the mind of Christendom been trained and illumined by the literatures of Greece and Rome, which in moral purity, in elevation of sentiment, in breadth and depth of thought, in the knowledge of the laws of Nature, in scientific accuracy, in sympathy and tenderness, are altogether inferior to the best writings of our own day? It is a mistake to suppose that this is a material age in which the love of religion, of poetry, of art, of excellence of whatever kind, is dead. The love of what is best has never at any time been alive save in the hearts of the chosen few; and in such souls it burns now with as sweet and steady a glow as when Plato spoke, and the blessed Saviour uttered words of divine wisdom. Here and now, in and around us, there is the heavenly presence of budding life, of widening vision, of "new thoughts urgent as the growth of wings." Let us turn the white forehead of hope to the fair time, and deem no labor great by which we shall become less unfit to do the work of God and man.

"Nay, never falter; no great deed is done
By falterers who ask for certainty.
No good is certain but the steadfast mind,
The undivided will to seek the good:
'T is that compels the elements and wrings
A human music from the indifferent air.
The greatest gift the hero leaves his race
Is to have been a hero. Say we fail!
We feed the high tradition of the world
And leave our spirit in our children's breasts."

But to enter upon such a course of life with well-founded hope of success, we must be reverent and devout. The thrill of awe is, as Goethe says, the best thing humanity has. We must understand and feel that the visible is but the shadow of the invisible, that the soul has its roots in God, whose kingdom is within us. We must perceive that what we know, believe, admire, love, and yearn for makes our real life; that we are worth what we *are*, and not what we possess and use. We must be lovers of perfection, as the divine Saviour bids us become,—"Be ye perfect, even as your Father in heaven is perfect." We must be conscious of the immortal spirit which is ourself, and walk in the company of God and of just men made perfect, striving after light and purity and strength, which are of the soul. We must love the inward, the true, and the eternal rather than the outward and transitory. We must believe that in very truth we are akin to God, that God is in us, and we in him, and consequently that it is our first duty to follow after perfection, completeness of life, in thought, in love, and in conduct. As it is good to know, so is it good to be strong, to be patient, to be humble, to be helpful; so is it good to do right, though the deed should be our only reward.

But we are beset by all manner of temptations to turn aside from a high and noble way of living. The line of least resistance for us is the common highway of money-getters and place-winners; and the moment a man gives evidence of ability, the whole world urges him to put it to immediate use. Our public opinion identifies the good with the useful, all else is visionary and unreal. The average man controls us not only in politics, but in religion, in art, and in literature. To turn away from material good in order to gain spiritual and intellectual benefit is held to be evidence of a feeble or perverted understanding. If a man is eloquent, let him become a lawyer, a politician, or a preacher; if he have a talent for science, let him become a physician, a practical chemist, or a civil engineer; if he have skill in writing, let him become a journalist or a contributor to magazines. No one asks himself, What shall I do to gain wisdom, strength, virtue, completeness of life; but the universal question is, How shall I make a living, get money, position, notoriety? In our hearts we should rather have the riches of a Rothschild than the mind of Plato, the imagination of Shakespeare, or the soul of Saint Theresa. We believe the best is outside of us, that the aids to the most desirable kind of life are to be found in material and mechanical things. We talk with pride of our numbers, our institutions, our machines; we love the display and noise of life, are eager to mingle in crowds, to live in great cities, and to listen to exaggerated and declamatory speech. The soberness of wisdom, the humility of religion, the plainness of worth, are unattractive and unrecognized. We rush after material things, like hunters after game; and in the excitement of the chase our pulse grows quick, and our vision confused. We have lost the art of patient work and expectation. We are no more capable of living in our work, of making it the means of our growth and happiness. What we do, must be quickly done, must have immediate results. Our success in solving the political and social problems has spoiled us. When we hear of a man who has been prosperous for years, whom no misfortune has sobered and softened, we expect him to be narrow and supercilious; and in the same way, a prosperous people are exposed to the danger of becoming self-complacent and superficial. We exaggerate the importance of our own achievements and think that which we have accomplished is the best; whereas the wise hold what they have done in slight esteem, and think only of becoming themselves nobler and wiser. Instead of boasting of our civilization, because we have industrial and commercial prosperity, wealth and liberty, churches, schools, and newspapers, we ought to ask ourselves whether civilization does not imply something more and higher than this,—what kind of soul lives and loves and thinks in this environment? Instead of trying to persuade ourselves that we are the greatest and most enlightened people, would it not be worth while to ask ourselves, in a dispassionate temper, whether our best men and women are the most intellectual, the most interesting, and the most Christian men and women to be found in the world? Do they not lack repose, distinction, a sense for complete and harmonious living? Must we not still look to Europe for our best religious and philosophic thought, our best poetry, painting, music, and architecture? "Let the passion for America," says Emerson, "cast out the passion for Europe." This is desirable, but numbers and wealth will not bring it about. While the best is said and done in Europe, the better sort of Americans will look thither,—just as Europe looks to us for corn and cotton, or mechanical appliances. We have done much, and much that it was well to do. We have, as Matthew Arnold says, solved the political and social problems better than any other people, though we ourselves perceive that the solution is by no means final. The conditions of our life are favorable to the many. It is easier for a man to assert himself here, than it is or has ever been elsewhere. A little sense, a little energy, is all that any one needs to make himself independent and comfortable; and because success of this kind is so easy it threatens to absorb our whole life. They alone seem to be living worthily who are doing practical work, who are developing the natural wealth of the country, starting new enterprises and inventing new machines. The political problems which interest us are financial; schools are maintained and fostered because they protect and strengthen our institutions; religious beliefs are tolerated and encouraged because they are aids to morality,—and morality means sobriety, honesty, industry, which lead to thrift. Then there is an idea that religion is a conservative power, useful as a bulwark against the assaults of anti-social fanatics. Philosophy, poetry, and art are not considered seriously, because they are not seen to bear any clear relation to our institutions and temporal well-being. Opinion rules the wide world over; and in the face of this strong public opinion which lays stress chiefly upon external things,—the environment, the machinery of life,—and not upon spiritual and intellectual qualities, it is not easy to love knowledge and virtue for themselves, for the strength and beauty they give to the soul, for their power to build up the being which is a man's very self. It is rare that men have faith in what but few believe in; they are gregarious, and need the encouragement that comes of having aims and hopes of which the millions approve.

The predominance of the average man, of which our public opinion is the result, puts other obstacles in the way of culture. It makes us self-complacent, easily satisfied with what we perform. A representative man will become a lawyer, a soldier, a merchant, a legislator, an author, in turns, as occasion offers, and he has no doubt of his sufficiency; because average work is all that is expected of any one. To be able to do anything fairly well seems to us a more desirable accomplishment than to be able to do some one thing better than anybody else. But this is a view which only those may take who live in an imperfectly developed society. As men become more cultivated, they more and more want only the best; and the noblest natures feel the desire to do their best, not with their actual power, but with the skill which forty or fifty years of discipline and effort might give them. They are laborious; they are patient; they persevere in one direction; they believe that if they but continue to observe, to think, to read, to compare, and to express in plain words what they know, their power of seeing and of uttering will continue to grow. The charm of increasing faculty in an infinite world sways and controls them. They never know enough; they are never able to say well enough what they know; and so they grow old still learning many things. They work in a spirit wholly different from that of the common man, who if he get through with what he has in hand is satisfied. They have an artist's sense of perfection; and like Virgil would burn the works which if they once escape their own hands, the world will never permit to perish.

It is hard to resist when many invite to utterance; and with us whoever has ability is urged to put himself forward, and consequently to dissipate in crude performances energies which if employed in self-culture might make of him a philosopher, a poet, or a man of science. As it is easier to act than to think, the multitude of course will be only talkers, writers, and performers; but a great and civilized people must have at least a few men who take rank with the profound thinkers and finished scholars of the world. No lover of America can help thinking it undesirable that any one should be able to say of us with truth, what Locke has said, "The Americans are not all born with worse understandings than the Europeans, though we see none of them have such reaches in the arts and sciences." It is our aim to create the highest civilization; but the highest civilization is favorable to the highest life, which implies and requires more than the possession of material things. Conduct is necessary, knowledge is necessary, beauty is necessary, manners are necessary, and a civilized people must develop life in all these directions, and as far as such a thing is possible, harmoniously. Whoever excels in conduct, or in knowledge, or in a sense for the beautiful, or in manners, helps to raise the standard of living,—helps to give worth, dignity, charm, and refinement to life. It is hard to take interest in a people who have no profound thinkers, no great artists, no accomplished scholars, for only such men can lift a people above the provincial spirit, and bring them into conscious relationship with former ages and the wide world. The rule of the people looks to something higher than opportunity for every man to have food and a home; to something more than putting a church, a school, and a newspaper at every man's door. Saints and heroes, philosophers and poets, are a people's glory. They give us nobler loves, higher thoughts, diviner aims. They show us how like a god man may become; and political and social institutions which make saints and heroes, philosophers and poets, impossible, can have but inferior value. And there is some radical wrong where the noblest manhood and womanhood are not appreciated and reverenced. Not to recognize genuine worth is the mark of a superficial and vulgar character. The servile spirit has no conception of the heroic nature; and they who measure life by material standards, do not perceive the infinite which is in man and which makes him godlike. A few only in any age or nation love the best, follow after ideal aims; but when these few are wanting, all life becomes common-place, and the millions pass from the cradle to the grave and leave no lasting impression upon the world.

The practical turn of mind which finds expression in our commercial and industrial achievements, makes itself felt also in our intellectual activity, and those among us who have knowledge and power of utterance are expected, almost required, to throw themselves into the breakers of controversy, to discuss the hundred political, social, religious, financial, sanitary, and educational problems which are ever waiting to be solved. Let them enter the lists, let them take sides, let them strive to see clear in an atmosphere of smoke and fog; and not to do this is, in the estimation of the many, to be a dreamer, a dilettante, a thinker to no purpose. But this is precisely what those who seek to cultivate themselves, who seek to learn and communicate the best that is known, ought not to do. They should live in a serene air, in a world of tranquillity and peace, where the soul is not troubled by contention, where the view is not perturbed by passion. They should have leisure, which is the original meaning of school and scholar; for the mind, like the soul, is refreshed and strengthened by quiet meditation. Its improvement is slow, is imperceptible often; its training is the result of delicate methods which require patience and perseverance, faith in ideals, and a constant looking to the all-perfect Infinite; and to throw it into the noise and confusion of the busy excited world of practical affairs is to stunt and warp its growth. We do not hitch a race-horse to the plough, nor should we ask the best intellects to do the common work of which every man is capable. They render the best service, when living in communion with the highest and most cultivated minds of the past and present, they learn and teach the way of looking and thinking, of behaving and doing, which has been followed by the greatest and noblest of the race. Political and social questions are forever changing; views which commend themselves to-day will in a few years seem absurd; measures which are thought to be of vital importance will grow to be inapplicable. To talk and write about such things is well,—may help to prevent stagnation and corruption in public life; but they exercise altogether a higher office, who live in the presence of what is permanently true and good and beautiful, who believe in ideal aims and ends and prevent the masses from losing sight of what constitutes man's real worth. They do what they alone can do, whereas the practical and the useful may be any one's work. They may not, of course, isolate themselves; on the contrary they must live closer than other men not only to God and Nature, but also to the past and present history of their country and of mankind. They study the movements of the age, but they study them in a philosophic and not in a partisan spirit. They seek to know, not what is popular, but what is right and good; and they often see clearly where the view of others is uncertain and confused. Encouragements and rewards are not necessary for them, for they are drawn to the knowledge and love of the best by irresistible attractions, and the more they learn and love the more beneficent and joy-giving does their life become. Their aims and ends are in harmony with the highest reason and the highest faith. The world they live in abides; and if they are neglected or forgotten now, they can wait, for truth and goodness and beauty can never lose their power or their charm.

> "The worthiest poets have remained uncrowned
> Till death has bleached their foreheads to the bone."

Chapter V.

Self-Culture.

There is
One great society alone on earth
The noble Living and the noble Dead.

WORDSWORTH.

The passion for truth and for the culture which makes its possession possible is not rightly felt by the heart of boy or of youth; it is the man's passion, and its power over him is most irresistibly asserted when outward restraint has been removed, when escaping from the control of parents and teachers he is left to himself to shape his course and seek his own ends. When his companions have finished their studies he feels that his own are now properly only about to begin; when they are dreaming of liberty and pleasure, of wealth and success, of the world and its honors, his mind is haunted by the mystery of God and Nature, by visions of dimly discerned truth and beauty which he must follow whithersoever they lead; and already he perceives that wisdom comes to those alone who toil and cease not from labor, who suffer and are patient. Hitherto he has learned the lessons given him by teachers appointed by others; henceforth he is himself to choose his instructors. As once, half-unconscious, he played in the smile or frown of Nature, and drank knowledge with delight, so now in the world of man's thought, hope, and love, he is, with deliberate purpose, to seek what is good for the nourishment of his soul. Happy is he, for nearly all men toil and suffer that they may live; but he is also to have time to labor, to make life intelligent and fair. He must know not only what the blind atoms are doing, but what saints, sages, and heroes have loved, thought, and done. He will still keep close to Nature who, though she utters myriad sounds, never speaks a human word; but he will also lend his ear to the voice of wisdom which lies asleep in books, and to sympathetic minds whispers from other worlds whatever high or holy truth has consecrated the life of man. His guiding thought must be how to make the work by which he maintains himself in the world subserve moral and intellectual ends; for his aim is not merely or chiefly to have goods, but to be wise and good, and therefore to build up within himself the power of conduct and the power of intelligence which makes man human, and distinguishes him from whatever else on earth has life.

It is our indolence and frivolity that make routine duties, however distracting or importunate, incompatible with the serious application which the work of self-culture demands; but we are by nature indolent and frivolous, and only education can make us earnest and laborious. None but a cultivated mind can understand that if the whole human race could be turned loose, to eat and drink and play like thoughtless children, life would become meaningless; that a paradise in which work should not be necessary would become wearisome. The progress of the race is the result of effort, physical, religious, moral, and intellectual; and the advance of individuals is proportional to their exertion. Nature herself pushes the young to bodily exercise; but though activity is for them a kind of necessity, only the discipline of habit will lead them to prefer labor to idleness; and they will not even use their senses properly unless they are taught to look and to listen,—just as they are taught to walk and to ride. The habit of manual labor, as it is directly related to the animal existence to which man is prone, and supplies the physical wants whose urgency is most keenly felt, is acquired with least difficulty, and it prepares the way for moral and intellectual life; but it especially favors the life which has regard to temporal ends and conduces to comfort and well-being. They whose instrument is the brain rarely aim at anything higher than wealth and position; and if they become rich and prominent, they remain narrow and uninteresting. They talk of progress, of new inventions and discoveries, and they neglect to improve themselves; they boast of the greatness of their country, while their real world is one of vulgar thought and desire; they take interest in what seems to concern the general welfare, but fail to make themselves centres of light and love. What is worse they have the conceit of wisdom,—they lack reverence; they are impatient, and must have at once what they seek. But the better among us see the insufficiency of the popular aims, and begin to yearn for something other than a life of politics, newspapers, and financial enterprise. They desire to know and love the best that is known, and they are willing to be poor and obscure, if they may but gain entrance into this higher world. "I shall ever consider myself," says Descartes, "more obliged to those who leave me to my leisure, than I should to any who might offer me the most honorable employments." This is the thought of every true student and lover of wisdom; for he feels that whatever a man's occupation may be, his business is to improve his mind and to form his character. He desires not to be known and appreciated, but to know and appreciate; not to *have* more, but to *be* more; not to have friends, but to be the friend of man,—which he is when he is the lover of truth. He turns from vulgar pleasures as he turns from pain, because both pleasure and pain in fastening the soul to the body deprive it of freedom and hinder the play of the mind.

> He loves the best with single heart
> And without thought what gifts it bring.

Unless one have deep faith in the good of culture he will easily become discouraged in the work which is here urged upon him. He must be drawn to the love of intellectual excellence by an attraction such as a poet feels in the presence of beauty; he must believe in it as a miser believes in gold; he must seek it as a lover seeks the beloved. Our wants determine our pleasures, and they who have no intellectual cravings feel not the need of exercise of mind. They are born and remain inferior. They are content with the world which seems to be real, forgetting the higher one, which alone is real; they are not urged to the intellectual life by irresistible instincts. They are discouraged by difficulties, thwarted by obstacles which lie in the path of all who strive to move forward and to gain higher planes. It is not possible to advance except along the road of toil, of struggle, and of suffering. We cannot emerge even from childish ignorance and weakness without experiencing a sense of loss. Mental work in the beginning and for a long time is weariness, is little better than drudgery. We labor, and there seems to be no gain; we study and there seems to be no increase of knowledge or power; and if we persevere, we are led by faith and hope, not by any clear perception of the result of persistent application. Genius itself is not exempt from this law. Poets and artists work with an intensity unknown to others, and are distinguished by their faith in the power of labor. The consummate musician must practise for hours, day by day, year in and year out. The brain is the most delicate and the finest of instruments, and it is vain to imagine that anything else than ceaseless, patient effort will enable us to use it with perfect skill; indeed, it is only after long study that we become capable of understanding what the perfection of the intellect is, that we become capable of discerning what is excellent, beautiful, and true in style and thought.

Discouragement and weariness will, again and again, suggest doubts concerning the wisdom of this ceaseless effort to improve one's self. Why persist in the pursuit of what can never be completely attained? Why toil to gain what the mass of men neither admire nor love? Why wear out life in a course of action which leads neither to wealth nor honors? Why turn away from pleasures which lie near us to follow after ideal things? These are questions which force themselves upon us; and it requires faith and courage not to be shaken by this sophistry. Visions of ideal life float before young eyes, and if to be attracted by what is high and fair were enough, it were not difficult to be saint, sage, or hero; but when we perceive that the way to the best is the road of toil and drudgery, that we must labor long and accomplish little, wander far and doubt our progress, must suffer much and feel misgivings whether it is not in vain,—then only the noblest and the bravest still push forward in obedience to inward law. The ideal of culture appeals to them with irresistible force. They consent to lack wealth, and the approval of friends and the world's applause; they are willing to turn away when fair hands hold out the cup of pleasure, when bright eyes and smiling lips woo to indulgence. If, you ask, How long? They answer, Until we die! They are lovers of wisdom and do not trust to hope of temporal reward. Their aim is light and purity of mind and heart; these they would not barter for comfort and position. As saints, while doing the common work of men, walk uplifted to worlds invisible, so they, amid the noise and distractions of life still hear the appealing voice of truth; and as parted lovers dream only of the hour when they shall meet again, so these chosen spirits, in the midst of whatever cares and labors, turn to the time when thought shall people their solitude as with the presence of angels. They hear heavenly voices asking, Why stay ye on the earth, unless to grow? Vanity, frivolity, and fickleness die within them; and they grow to be humble and courageous, disinterested and laborious, strong and persevering. The cultivation of their higher nature becomes the law of their life; and the sense of duty, "stern daughter of the voice of God," which of all motives that sway the heart, best stands the test of reason, becomes their guide and support. Thus culture, which looks to the Infinite and All-wise as to its ideal, rests upon the basis of morality and religion.

To think is difficult, and they who wish to grow in power of thought must hoard their strength. Excess, of whatever kind, is a waste of intellectual force. The weakness of men of genius has impoverished the world. Sensual indulgence diminishes spiritual insight; it perverts reason, and deadens love; it enfeebles the physical man, and weakens the organs of sense, which are the avenues of the soul. The higher self is developed harmoniously only when it springs from a healthful body. It is the lack of moral balance which makes genius akin to madness. Nothing is so sane as reason, and great minds fall from truth only when they fail in the strength which comes of righteous conduct.

Let the lover of wisdom then strive to live in a healthy body that his senses may report truly of the universe in which he dwells. But this is not easy; for mental labor exhausts, and if the vital forces are still further diminished by dissipation, disease and premature decay of the intellectual faculties will be the result. The ideal of culture embraces the whole man, physical, moral, religious, and intellectual; and the loss of health or morality or faith cannot but impede the harmonious development of the mind itself. Passion is the foe of reason, and may easily become strong enough to extinguish its light. He who wishes to educate himself must learn to resist the desires of his lower nature, which if indulged deaden sensibility, weaken the will, take from the imagination its freshness, and from the heart the power of loving. The task he has set himself is arduous, and he cannot have too much energy, too much warmth of soul, too much capacity for labor. Let him not waste, like a mere animal, the strength which was given him that he might learn to know and love infinite truth and beauty. The dwelling with one's self and with thoughts of what is true and high, which is an essential condition of mental growth, is impossible when the sanctuary of the soul is filled with unclean images. Intellectual honesty, the disinterested love of truth, without which no progress can be made, will hardly be found in those who are the slaves of unworthy passions. The more religious a man is, the more does he believe in the worth and sacredness of truth, and the more willing does he become to throw all his energies with persevering diligence into the work of self-improvement. They who fail to see in the universe an all-wise, all-holy, and all-powerful Being, from whom are all things and to whom all things turn, easily come to doubt whether it holds anything of true worth. History teaches this, and it requires little reflection to perceive that it must be so. Of the Solitary, Wordsworth says,—

"But in despite
Of all this outside bravery, within
He neither felt encouragement nor hope;
For moral dignity and strength of mind
Were wanting, and simplicity of life
And reverence for himself; and, last and best,
Confiding thoughts, through love and fear of Him
Before whose sight the troubles of this world
Are vain."

The corrupt and the ignorant easily learn to feel contempt, but the scholar is reverent. He moves in the midst of infinite worlds, and knows that the least is part of the whole.

Now, how shall he who is resolved to educate himself set about his work? What advice shall be given him? What rules shall be made for him that he may not waste time and energy? He who yearns for the cultivation of mind which makes wisdom possible must work his way to the light. All intellectual men strive to educate themselves, but each one strives in a different way. They all aim at insight rather than information, at the perfect use of their faculties rather than learning. The power to see things as they are, is what they want; and therefore they look, observe, examine, compare, analyze, meditate, read, and write. And they keep doing this day by day; and the longer they work, the more attractive their work grows to be. Descartes, who is a typical lover of the intellectual life, looked upon himself simply as a thinking being, and gave all his thought to the cultivation of his higher faculties in the hope that he might finally discover some truth which would bring blessings to men. He had no thought of literary fame, published little, and sedulously avoided whatever might bring him into notoriety. "Those," he says, "who wish to know how to speak of everything and to acquire a reputation for learning, will succeed most easily if they content themselves with the semblance of truth, which may readily be found." The love of truth is the mark of the real student. What is, is; it is man's business to know it. He is the foe of pretense; sham for him means shame. He will have sound knowledge; he will do his work well; whether men shall applaud or reward him for it, is a foreign consideration. He obeys an inward law, and the praise of those who cannot understand him sounds to him like mockery. True thought, like right conduct, is its own reward. To see truth and to love it is enough,—is more than to have the worship of the world. The important thing is to be a man, to have a serious purpose, to be in earnest, to yearn for what is good and holy; and without this the culture of the intellect will not avail.

We must build upon the broad foundation of man's life, and not upon any special faculty. The merely literary man is often the most pitiful of men,—able, it may be, to do little else than complain that his merits are not recognized. Let it not be imagined then that the lover of wisdom, the follower of intellectual good, should propose to himself a literary career. He may of course be or become a man of letters, but this is incidental to his life-purpose, which is to develop within himself the power of knowing and loving. He will learn to think rightly and to act well, first of all; for he knows that a man's writing cannot be worth more than he himself is worth. He is a seeker after truth and perfection; and understanding at the price of what countless labors these may be hoped for, he is slow to imagine that words of his may be of help to others.

Observation, reading, and writing are the chief means by which thought is stimulated, the mind developed, and the intellect cultivated. The habit of looking and the habit of thinking are closely related. A man thinks as he sees; and for a mind like Shakespeare's, for instance, observation is almost the only thing that is necessary for its development. The boundless world breaks in upon him with creative force. His sympathy is universal, and therefore so is his interest. He sees the like in the unlike, the differences in things which are similar. Every little bird and every little flower are known to him. He contemplates Falstaff and Poor Tom with as much interest as though they were Hamlet and King Lear. In all original minds the power of observation is great. It is the chief source of our earliest knowledge, of that which touches us most nearly and most deeply colors the imagination. When the boy is wandering through fields, sitting in the shade of trees, or lying on the banks of murmuring streams, he is not only learning more delightful things than books will ever teach him, but he is also acquiring the habit of attention, of looking at what he sees, which nowhere else can be gotten in so natural and pleasant a way. Hence the best minds have either been born in the country or have passed there some of their early years. Unless we have first learned to look with the eye, we shall never learn to look with the mind. They who walk unmoved beneath the starlit heavens, or by the ever-moving ocean, or amid the silent mountains; who do not find, like Wordsworth, that the meanest flower that blows gives thoughts which often lie too deep for tears, will not derive great help from the world of books. But in the world of books the intellectual must also make themselves at home and live, must thence draw nourishment, light, wisdom, strength, for there as nowhere else the mind of man has stamped its image; and there the thoughts of the master spirits still breathe, still glow with truth and beauty. The best books are powers

> "Forever to be hallowed; only less,
> For what we are and what we may become,
> Than Nature's self, which is the breath of God,
> Or his pure Word, by miracle revealed."

But it is as difficult to know books as to know men. There are but few men who can be of intellectual service to us; and there are but few books which stimulate and nourish the mind. The best books are, as Milton says, "the precious life-blood of a master spirit;" and it is absurd to suppose that they will reveal their secret to every chance comer, to every heedless reader. As it takes a hero to know a hero, so only an awakened mind can love and understand the great thinkers. The reading of the ignorant is chiefly a mechanical proceeding; and, indeed, for men in general reading is little better than waste of time. Their reading, like their conversation, leaves them what they were, or worse. The mass of printed matter has no greater value from an intellectual point of view at least than the wide ever-flowing stream of talk; and for the multitude it is all the same whether they gossip and complain, or read and nod. However much they read, they remain unintelligent; what knowledge they gain is fragmentary, unreal; they learn merely enough to talk about what they do not understand. We may of course read for entertainment, as we may talk for entertainment; but this is merely a recreation of the mind, which is good only because it rests and prepares us for work. The wise read books to be enlightened, uplifted, and inspired. Their reading is a labor in which every faculty of the mind is awake and active. They are attentive; they weigh, compare, judge. They re-create within their own minds the images produced by the author; they seek to enter into his inmost thought; they admire each well-turned phrase, each happy epithet; they walk with him, and make themselves at home in the wonderland which his genius has called into being; past centuries rise before them, and they almost forget that they did not hear Plato discourse in the Academy, or stroll with Horace along the Sacred Way. As they are brought thus intimately into the company of the noblest minds, they think as they thought, feel as they felt, and so are enlightened and inspired. They drink the spirit of the mighty dead, and gradually come to live in a higher and richer world. The best in life and literature is seen to be such only by those who have made themselves worthy of the heavenly vision; and once we have learned to love the few real books of the world, or rather what in these few is eternally true and beautiful, we breathe the atmosphere of the intellectual life. What is frivolous, or false, or vulgar can no longer please us; having seen and loved what is high we may not sink to the lower.

Knowledge may be useful, and yet have little power to nourish, train, and enlarge the mind, and it is its disciplinary and educational value which we are here considering. Medicine for a physician, law for an attorney, theology for a clergyman, is the most useful knowledge; but they are not therefore the best means of intellectual culture. Natural science, though it is most useful, ministering as it does in a thousand ways and with ever-increasing efficacy to our wants and comforts, has but an inferior educational power. Acquaintance with the uniform co-existences and sequences of phenomena is not a mental tonic. Such knowledge not only leaves us unmoved,—it has a tendency even to fetter the free play of the mind and to chill the imagination. It unweaves the rainbow, and leaves us the dead chemical elements. The information we have gained is practical, but it does not exalt the soul or render us more keenly alive to the divine beauty which rests on Nature's face. It does not enable us, as does the knowledge of literature and history, to participate in the conscious life of the race. It makes no appeal to our nobler human instincts. There is no book on natural science, nor can there ever be one, which may take a place among the few immortal works which men never cease to read and love. Physical science has its own domain, and its study will continue to enrich the world, to make specialists of a hundred kinds; but it never can take the place of literature and history as a means of culture; and as an educational force its value is greatest when it is studied not experimentally, but as literature,—though of course, every cultivated man should be familiar with the inductive method, and should receive consequently a certain scientific training.

History, in bringing us into the presence of the greatest men and in showing us their mightiest achievements, rouses our whole being. It sets the mind aglow, awakens enthusiasm, and fires the imagination. It makes us feel how blessed a thing it is "to scorn delights and live laborious days;" how divine to perish in bringing truth and holiness to men. We commingle with the makers of the world; we hear them speak and see them act; we catch the spirit of their lofty purpose, their high courage, their noble eloquence. When we drink deeply of the wisdom which history teaches, we come to understand that truth and justice, heroism and religion, which are the virtues of the greatest men, may be ours as easily as theirs; that opportunity for true men is ever present, and that the task set for each one of us is as sacred and important as any which has ever been entrusted to the human mind and will. Our thought is widened, our hearts are strengthened, and we come to feel that it shall be well for others that we too have lived. When we have learned to be at home with lofty and generous natures, the heroic mood becomes natural to us.

There are of course but few histories which have this tonic effect upon the mind and the will, but with these the lover of culture should make himself familiar. Each one must find the book he needs; and though he should find no help in a volume which time and the consent of the learned have consecrated, let him not be discouraged, but continue to seek and to read until he meet with the author who fills his soul with joy and opens to his wondering eyes visions of new worlds. To love any great book so that we read it—or at least those portions of it which especially appeal to us—many times, and always with new pleasure (as a mother never wearies of looking upon her child), until the thought and style of the author become almost our own, is to learn the secret of self-education; for he who understands and loves one great book is sure to find his way to the love and knowledge of other works of genius. He will not read chiefly to gain information, but he will read for exaltation of spirit, for enlightenment, for strength of soul, for the help which springs from contact with generous and awakened minds. He will mark his favorite passages and refer to them often, as one loves to revisit places where he has been happy; and these very pencil-marks will become dear to him as tokens of truth revealed, of wisdom gained, of joy bestowed. The best reading is that which most profoundly stimulates thought, which brings our own minds into active, conscious communion with the mind of the author; and hence the best poetry is the most efficacious and the most delightful aid to mental improvement.

Poetry is, as Aristotle says, the most philosophic of all writing. It is also the writing which is most instinct with passion, with life. It springs from intense thought and feeling, and bears within itself the power to call forth thought and feeling. It is thought transfused with the glow of emotion, and consequently thought made beautiful, attractive, contagious. It is, to quote Wordsworth, "the breath and finer spirit of all knowledge; it is the impassioned expression which is in the countenance of all science." The poet has more enthusiasm and tenderness than other men, a more sensitive soul, a more comprehensive mind. His wider sympathy gives him greater insight; and his power to see absent things as though they were present enables him to bring the distant and the past before our eyes, to make them live again in a new and immortal world; he stimulates the whole mind and appeals to every faculty of the soul. The greatest philosophers are, like Plato, poets too; and unless the historian is also a poet, there is no inspiration, no life in what he writes. It is as superficial and vulgar to sneer at poetry as to sneer at religion; and they alone are mockers who have eyes but for some counterfeit. To be able to read a true poet is not a gift of Nature; it is a faculty to be acquired. He creates, as Wordsworth says, the taste by which he is appreciated. To imagine we may read him as we read a frivolous novel is absurd; it may well happen we shall see no truth or beauty in him until patient study has made it plain. It often takes the world a hundred years or more to recognize a great poet; and a knowledge of his worth can be had by the student only at the price of patient labor. Wordsworth will attract scarcely any one at the first glance; the great number of readers will soon weary of him and throw him aside; but those who learn to understand him find in his writings treasures above all price. There are but a few great poems in the literatures of the different nations, but he who wishes to have a cultivated mind must, at the cost of whatever time and labor, make himself familiar with them; for there alone are found the best thoughts clothed in fittest words; there alone are rightly portrayed the noblest characters; there alone is the world of men and things transfigured by the imagination and illumined by the pure light of the mind. True poets help us to see, they teach us to admire, they lift our thoughts, they appeal to our higher nature; they give us nobler loves, more exalted aims, more spiritual purposes; they make us feel that to live for money or place is to lead a narrow and a slavish life; and to men around whom the fetters of material and hardening cares are growing, they cry and bid them—

> "Look abroad
> And see to what fair countries they are bound."

But even the greatest poets have weaknesses, and are great only by comparison. There is not one who however he may enchant and strengthen, does not also disappoint us. The perfect poet the future will bring; and to his coming we shall look with more eager expectation than if we foresaw man dowered with wings. The elevation we forebode is of the soul, not of the body. Progress we have already made. It is no longer possible for a true poet to sing of sensual delights; the man he creates is now no more the slave "of low ambition or distempered love." His theme is rather—

> "No other than the heart of man
> As found among the best of those who live,
> Not unexalted by religious faith,
> Nor uninformed by books, good books, though few,
> In Nature's presence."

Writing is as great an aid to the cultivation of the mind as reading. It is indeed indispensable, and the accuracy of thought and expression of which Bacon speaks, is but one of its good results. "By writing," says Saint Augustine, "I have learned many things which nothing else had taught me." There is, of course, no question here of writing for publication. To do this no one should be urged. The farther we are from all thought of readers, the nearer are we to truth; and once an author has published, a sort of madness comes over him, and he seems to be doing nothing unless he continue to publish. The truly intellectual man leads an interior life; he dwells habitually in the presence of God, of Nature, and of his own soul; he swims in a current of ideas, looks out upon a world of truth and beauty; he would rather gain some new vision of the eternal reality than to have a mountain of gold or the suffrages of a whole people. The great hindrance is lack of the power of prolonged attention, of sustained thought; and this the habit of serious writing gives. But the habit itself is difficult to acquire. At first in attempting to write we are discouraged to find how crude, how unreal, how little within our control our knowledge is; and it will often happen that we shall simply hold the pen in idleness, either because we find nothing to write, or because the proper way to express what we think eludes our efforts. When this happens day after day, the temptation will come to abandon our purpose, and to seek easier and less effective means of developing mental strength, or else we shall write carelessly and without thought, which is even a greater evil than not to write at all. In the writing of which I am thinking there is no question of style, of what critics and readers will say; all that is asked is that we apply our minds to things as they appear to us, and put in plain words what we see. Thus our style will become the expression of our thought and life. It will be the outgrowth of a natural method, and consequently will have genuine worth. What is written in this way should be preserved, not that others may see it, but that we ourselves by comparing our earlier with our later essays may be encouraged by the evidence of improvement. It is not necessary to make choice of a subject,—whatever interests us is a fit theme; and if nothing should happen specially to interest us, by writing we shall gain interest in many things.

The method here proposed requires serious application, perseverance, diligence: it is difficult; but they who have the courage to continue to write, undeterred by difficulties, will gain more than they hope for. They will grow in strength, in accuracy, in pliancy, in openness of mind; they will become capable of profound and just views, and will gradually rise to worlds of truth and beauty of which the common man does not dream. And it will frequently happen that there will be permanent value in what is written not to please the crowd or to flatter a capricious public opinion, or to win gold or applause, but simply in the presence of God and one's own soul to bear witness to truth. As the painter takes pallet and brush, the musician his instrument, each to perfect himself in his art, so he who desires to learn how to think should take the pen, and day by day write something of the truth and love, the hope and faith, which make him a living man.

Chapter VI.

Growth and Duty.

Why stay we on the earth unless to grow?

BROWNING.

What life is in itself we do not know, any more than we know what matter is in itself; but we know something of the properties of matter, and we also have some knowledge of the laws of life. Here it is sufficient to call attention to the law of growth, through which the living receive the power of self-development,—of bringing their endowments into act, of building up the being which they are. Whatever living thing is strong or beautiful has been made so by growth, since life begins in darkness and impotence. To grow is to be fresh and joyous. Hence the spring is the glad time; for the earth itself then seems to renew its youth, and enter on a fairer life. The growing grass, the budding leaves, the sprouting corn, coming as with unheard shout from regions of the dead, fill us with happy thoughts, because in them we behold the vigor of life, bringing promise of higher things.

Nature herself seems to rejoice in this vital energy; for the insects hum, the birds sing, the lambs skip, and the very brooks give forth a merry sound. Growth leads us through Wonderland. It touches the germs lying in darkness, and the myriad forms of life spring to view; the mists are lifted from the valleys, and flowers bloom and shed fragrance through the air. Only the growing—those who each moment are becoming something more than they were—feel the worth and joyousness of life. Upon the youth nothing palls, for he is himself day by day rising into higher and wider worlds. To grow is to have faith, hope, courage.

The boy who has become able to do what a while ago was impossible to him, easily believes that nothing is impossible; and as his powers unfold, his self-confidence is nourished; he exults in the consciousness of increasing strength, and cannot in any way be made to understand the doubts and faint-heartedness of men who have ceased to grow. Each hour he puts off some impotence, and why shall he not have faith in his destiny, and feel that he shall yet grow to be poet, orator, hero, or what you will that is great and noble? And as he delights in life, we take delight in him.

In the same way a young race of people possesses a magic charm. Homer's heroes are barbarians; but they are inspiring, because they belong to a growing race, and we see in them the budding promise of the day when Alexander's sword shall conquer the world; when Plato shall teach the philosophy which all men who think must know; and when Pericles shall bid the arts blossom in a perfection which is the despair of succeeding generations. And so in the Middle Ages there is barbarism enough, with its lawlessness and ignorance; but there is also faith, courage, strength, which tell of youth, and point to a time of mature faculty and high achievement. There is the rich purple dawn which shall grow into the full day of our modern life.

Here in this New World we are the new people, in whose growth what highest hopes, what heavenly promises lie! All the nations which are moving forward, are moving in directions in which we have gone before them,—to larger political and religious liberty; to wider and more general education; to the destroying of privilege and the disestablishment of churches; to the recognition of the equal rights not only of all men, but of all men and women.

We also lead the way in the revolution which has been set in motion by the application of science to mechanical purposes, one of the results of which is seen in the industrial and commercial miracles of the present century. It is our vigorous growth which makes us the most interesting and attractive of the modern peoples. For whether men love us, or whether they hate us, they find it impossible to ignore us, unless they wish to argue themselves unknown; and the millions who yearn for freedom and opportunity turn first of all to us.

But observant minds, however much they may love America, however great their faith in popular government may be, cannot contemplate our actual condition without a sense of disquietude; for there are aspects of our social evolution which sadden and depress even the most patriotic and loyal hearts. It would seem, for instance, that with us, while the multitude are made comfortable and keen-witted, the individual remains common-place and weak; so that on all sides people are beginning to ask themselves what is the good of all this money and machinery if the race of godlike men is to die out, or indeed if the result is not to be some nobler and better sort of man than the one with whom we have all along been familiar. Is not the yearning for divine men inborn? In the heroic ages such men were worshipped as gods, and one of the calamities of times of degeneracy is the dying out of faith in the worth of true manhood caused by the disappearance of superior men. Such men alone are memorable, and give to history its inspiring and educating power. The ruins of Athens and Rome, the cathedrals and castles of Europe, uplift and strengthen the heart, because they bid us reflect what thoughts and hopes were theirs who thus could build.

How quickly kings and peasants, millionaires and paupers, become a common, undistinguished crowd! But the hero, the poet, the saint, defy the ages and remain luminous and separate like stars. They—

> "Waged contention with their time's decay,
> And of the past are all that cannot pass away."

The soul, which makes man immortal, has alone the power to make him beneficent and beautiful.

But in this highest kind of man, in whom soul—that is, faith, hope, love, courage, intellect—is supreme, we Americans, who are on the crest of the topmost waves of the stream of tendency, are not rich. We have our popular heroes; but so has every petty people, every tribe its heroes. The dithyrambic prose in which it is the fashion to celebrate our conspicuous men has a hollow sound, very like cant. A marvellous development of wealth and numbers has taken place in America; but what American—poet, philosopher, scientist, warrior, ruler, saint—is there who can take his place with the foremost men of all this world? The American people seem still to be somewhat in the position of our new millionaires: their fortune is above them, overshadows, and oppresses them. They live in fine houses, and have common thoughts; they have costly libraries, and cheap culture; and their rich clothing poorly hides their coarse breeding. Nor does the tendency seem to be toward a nobler type of manhood.

The leaders of the Revolution, the framers of the Federal Constitution, the men who contended for State-rights, and still more those who led in the great struggle for human rights were of stronger and nobler mould than the politicians who now crowd the halls of Congress. The promise of a literature which a generation ago budded forth in New England was, it appears, delusive. What a sad book is not that recently issued from the press on the poets of America! It is the chapter on snakes in Ireland which we have all read,—there are none. And are not our literary men whom it is possible to admire and love either dead or old enough to die?

All this, however, need not be cause for discouragement, if in the generations which are springing up around us, and which are soon to enter upon the scene of active life, we could discover the boundless confidence, the high courage, the noble sentiments, which make the faults of youth more attractive than the formal virtues of a maturer age. But youth seems about to disappear from our life, to leave only children and men. For a true youth the age of chivalry has not passed, nor has the age of faith, nor the age of poetry, nor the age of aught that is godlike and ideal. To our young men, however, high thoughts and heroic sentiments are what they are to a railroad president or a bank cashier,—mere nonsense. Life for them is wholly prosaic and without illusions. They transform ideas into interests, faith into a speculation, and love into a financial transaction. They have no vague yearnings for what cannot be; hardly have they any passions. They are cold and calculating. They deny themselves, and do not believe in self-denial; they are active, and do not love labor; they are energetic, and have no enthusiasm; they approach life with the hard, mechanical thoughts with which a scientist studies matter. Their one idea is success, and success for them is money. Money means power, it means leisure, it means self-indulgence, it means display; it means, in a word, the thousand comforts and luxuries which, in their opinion, constitute the good of life.

In aristocratic societies the young have had a passion for distinction. They have held it to be an excellent thing to belong to a noble family, to occupy an elevated position, to wear the glittering badges of birth and of office. In ages of religious faith they have been smitten with the love of divine ideals; they have yearned for God, and given all the strength of their hearts to make his will prevail. But to our youth distinction of birth is fictitious, and God is problematic; and so they are left face to face with material aims and ends; and of such aims and ends money is the universal equivalent.

Now, it could not ever occur to me to think of denying that the basis of human life, individual and social, is material. Matter is part of our nature; we are bedded in it, and by it are nourished. It is the instrument we must use even when we think and love, when we hope and pray. Upon this foundation our spiritual being is built; upon this foundation our social welfare rests.

Concern for material interests is one of the chief causes of human progress; since nothing else so stimulates to effort, and effort is the law of growth. The savage who has no conception of money, but is satisfied with what Nature provides, remains forever a savage. Habits of industry, of order, of punctuality, of economy and thrift, are, to a great extent, the result of our money-getting propensities. Our material wants are more urgent, more irresistible; they press more constantly upon us than any other; and those whom they fail to rouse to exertion are, as a rule, hopelessly given over to indolence and sloth. In the stimulus of these lower needs, then, is found the impulse which drives men to labor; and without labor welfare is not possible.

The poor must work, if they would drink and eat;
The weak must work, if they in strength would grow;
The ignorant must work, if they would know;
The sad must work, if they sweet joy would meet.

The strong must work, if they would shun defeat;
The rich must work, if they would flee from woe;
The proud must work, if they would upward go;
The brave must work, if they would not retreat.

So for all men the law of work is plain;
It gives them food, strength, knowledge, vict'ry, peace;
It makes joy possible, and lessens pain;
From passion's lawless power it wins release,
Confirms the heart, and widens reason's reign,
Makes men like God, whose work can never cease.

Whatever enables man to overcome his inborn love of ease is, in so far, the source of good. Now, money represents what more than anything else has this stimulating power. It is the equivalent of what we eat and drink, of the homes we live in, of the comforts with which we surround ourselves, of the independence which makes us free to go here or there, to do this or that,—to spend the winter where orange blossoms perfume the soft air, and the summer where ocean breezes quicken the pulse of life. It unlocks for us the treasury of the world, opens to our gaze whatever is sublime or beautiful; introduces us to the master-minds who live in their works; it leads us where orators declaim, and singers thrill the soul with ecstasy. Nay, more, with it we build churches, endow schools, and provide hospitals and asylums for the weak and helpless. It is, indeed, like a god of this nether world, holding dominion over many spheres of life and receiving the heart-worship of millions.

Yet, if we make money and its equivalents a life-purpose—the aim and end of our earthly hopes—our service becomes idolatry, and a blight falls upon the nobler self. Money is the equivalent of what is venal,—of all that may be bought or sold; but the best, the godlike, the distinctively human, cannot be bought or sold. A rich man can buy a wife, but not a woman's love; he can buy books, but not an appreciative mind; he can buy a pew, but not a pure conscience; he can buy men's votes and flattery, but not their respect. The money-world is visible, material, mechanical, external; the world of the soul, of the better self, is invisible, spiritual, vital. God's kingdom is within. What we have is not what we are; and the all-important thing is to be, and not to have. Our possessions belong to us only in a mechanical way. The poet's soul owns the stars and the moonlit heavens, the mountains and rivers, the flowers and the birds, more truly than a millionaire owns his bonds. What I know is mine, and what I love is mine; and as my knowledge widens and my love deepens, my life is enlarged and intensified. But, since all human knowledge is imperfect and narrow, the soul stretches forth the tendrils of faith and hope. Looking upon shadows, we believe in realities; possessing what is vain and empty, we trust to the future to bring what is full and complete.

All noble literature and life has its origin in regions where the mind sees but darkly; where faith is more potent than knowledge; where hope is larger than possession, and love mightier than sensation. The soul is dwarfed whenever it clings to what is palpable and plain, fixed and bounded. Its home is in worlds which cannot be measured and weighed. It has infinite hopes, and longings, and fears; lives in the conflux of immensities; bathes on shores where waves of boundless yearning break. Borne on the wings of time, it still feels that only what is eternal is real,—that what death can destroy is even now but a shadow. To it all outward things are formal, and what is less than God is hardly aught. In this mysterious, super-sensible world all true ideals originate, and such ideals are to human life as rain and sunshine to the corn by which it is nourished.

What hope for the future is there, then, when the young have no enthusiasm, no heavenly illusions, no divine aspirations, no faith that man may become godlike, more than poets have ever imagined, or philosophers dreamed?—when money, and what money buys, is the highest they know, and therefore the highest they are able to love?—when even the ambitious among them set out with the deliberate purpose of becoming the beggars of men's votes; of winning an office the chief worth of which, in their eyes, lies in its emoluments?—when even the glorious and far-sounding voice of fame for them means only the gabble and cackle of notoriety?

The only example which I can call to mind of an historic people whose ideals are altogether material and mechanical, is that of China. Are we, then, destined to become a sort of Chinese Empire, with three hundred millions of human beings, and not a divine man or woman?

Is what Carlyle says is hitherto our sole achievement—the bringing into existence of an almost incredible number of bores—is this to be the final outcome of our national life? Is the commonest man the only type which in a democratic society will in the end survive? Does universal equality mean universal inferiority? Are republican institutions fatal to noble personality? Are the people as little friendly to men of moral and intellectual superiority as they are to men of great wealth! Is their dislike of the millionaires but a symptom of their aversion to all who in any way are distinguished from the crowd? And is this the explanation of the blight which falls upon the imagination and the hearts of the young?

Ah! surely, we who have faith in human nature, who believe in freedom and in popular government, can never doubt what answer must be given to all these questions. A society which inevitably represses what is highest in the best sort of men is an evil society. A civilization which destroys faith in genius, in heroism, in sanctity, is the forerunner of barbarism. Individuality is man's noblest triumph over fate, his most heavenly assertion of the freedom of the soul; and a world in which individuality is made impossible is a slavish world. There man dwindles, becomes one of a multitude, the impersonal product of a general law; and all his godlike strength and beauty are lost. Is not one true poet more precious than a whole generation of millionaires; one philosopher of more worth than ten thousand members of Congress; one man who sees and loves God dearer than an army of able editors?

The greater our control of Nature becomes, the more its treasures are explored and utilized, the greater the need of strong personality to counteract the fatal force of matter. Just as men in tropical countries are overwhelmed and dwarfed by Nature's rich profusion, so in this age, in which industry and science have produced resources far beyond the power of unassisted Nature, only strong characters, marked individualities, can resist the influence of wealth and machinery, which tend to make man of less importance than that which he eats and wears,—to make him subordinate to the tools he uses.

From many sides personality, which is the fountain-head of worth, genius, and power, is menaced. The spirit of the time would deny that God is a Person, and holds man's personality in slight esteem, as not rooted in the soul, but in aggregated atoms. The whole social network, in whose meshes we are all caught, cripples and paralyzes individuality. We must belong to a party, to a society, to a ring, to a clique, and deliver up our living thought to these soulless entities. Or, if we remain aloof from such affiliation, we must have no honest conviction, no fixed principles, but fit our words to business and professional interests, and conform to the exigencies of the prevailing whim. The minister is hired to preach not what he believes, but what the people wish to hear; the congressman is elected to vote not in the light of his own mind, but in obedience to the dictates of those who send him; the newspaper circulates not because it is filled with words of truth and wisdom, but because it panders to the pruriency and prejudice of its patrons; and a book is popular in inverse ratio to its individuality and worth. Our National Library is filled with books which have copyright, but no other right, human or divine, to exist at all; and when one of us does succeed in asserting his personality, he usually only makes himself odd and ridiculous. He rushes into polygamous Mormonism, or buffoon revivalism, or shallow-minded atheism; nay, he will even become an anarchist, because a few men have too much money and too little soul. What we need is neither the absence of individuality nor a morbid individuality, but high and strong personalities.

If our country is to be great and forever memorable, something quite other than wealth and numbers will make it so. Were there but question of countless millions of dollars and people, then indeed the victory would already have been gained. If we are to serve the highest interests of mankind, and to mark an advance in human history, we must do more than establish universal suffrage, and teach every child to read and write. As true criticism deals only with men of genius or of the best talent, and takes no serious notice of mechanical writers and book-makers, so true history loses sight of nations whose only distinction lies in their riches and populousness.

The noblest and most gifted men and women are alone supremely interesting and abidingly memorable. We have already reached a point where we perceive the unreality of the importance which the chronicles have sought to give to mere kings and captains. If the king was a hero, we love him; but if he was a sot or a coward, his jewelled crown and purple robes leave him as unconsidered by us as the beggar in his rags. Whatever influence, favorable or unfavorable, democracy may exert to make easy or difficult the advent of the noblest kind of man, an age in which the people think and rule will strip from all sham greatness its trappings and tinsel. The parade hero and windy orator will be gazed at and applauded, but they are all the while transparent and contemptible. The scientific spirit, too, which now prevails, is the foe of all pretense; it looks at things in their naked reality, is concerned to get a view of the fact as it is, without a care whether it be a beautiful or an ugly, a sweet or a bitter truth. The fact is what it is, and nothing can be gained by believing it to be what it is not.

This is a most wise and human way of looking at things, if men will only not forget that the mind sees farther than the eye, that the heart feels deeper than the hand; and that where knowledge fails, faith is left; where possession is denied, hope remains. The young must enter upon their life-work with the conviction that only what is real is true, good, and beautiful; and that the unreal is altogether futile and vain.

Now, the most real thing for every man, if he is a man, is his own soul. His thought, his love, his faith, his hope, are but his soul thinking, loving, believing, hoping. His joy and misery are but his soul glad or sad. Hence, so far as we are able to see or argue, the essence of reality is spiritual; and since the soul is conscious that it is not the supreme reality, but is dependent, illumined by a truth higher than itself, nourished by a love larger than its own, it has a dim vision of the Infinite Being as essentially real and essentially spiritual. A living faith in this infinite spiritual reality is the fountain-head not only of religion, but of noble life. All wavering here is a symptom of psychic paralysis. When the infinite reality becomes questionable, then all things become material and vile. The world becomes a world of sight and sound, of taste and touch. The soul is poured through the senses and dissipated; the current of life stagnates, and grows fetid in sloughs and marshes. Minds for whom God is the Unknowable have no faith in knowledge at all, except as the equivalent of weight and measure, of taste and touch and smell.

Now, if all that may be known and desired is reduced to this material expression, how dull and beggarly does not life become,—mere atomic integration and disintegration, the poor human pneumatic-machine puffing along the dusty road of matter, bound and helpless and soulless as a clanking engine! No high life, in individuals or nations, is to be hoped for, unless it is enrooted in the infinite spiritual reality,—in God. It is forever indubitable that the highest is not material, and no argument is therefore needed to show that when spiritual ideals lose their power of attraction, life sinks to lower beds.

Sight is the noblest sense, and the starlit sky is the most sublime object we can behold. But what do we in reality see there? Only a kind of large tent, dimly lighted with gas jets. This is the noblest thing the noblest sense reveals. But let the soul appear, and the tent flies into invisible shreds; the heavens break open from abyss to abyss, still widening into limitless expanse, until imagination reels. The gas jets grow into suns, blazing since innumerable ages with unendurable light, and binding whole planetary systems into harmony and life. So infinitely does the soul transcend the senses! The world it lives in is boundless, eternal, sublime. This is its home; this the sphere in which it grows, and awakens to consciousness of kinship with God. This is the fathomless, shoreless abyss of being wherein it is plunged, from which it draws its life, its yearning for the absolute, its undying hope, its love of the best, its craving for immortality, its instinct for eternal things. To condemn it to work merely for money, for position, for applause, for pleasure, is to degrade it to the condition of a slave. It is as though we should take some supreme poet or hero and bid him break stones or grind corn,—he who has the faculty to give to truth its divinest form, and to lift the hearts of nations to the love of heavenly things.

Whatever our lot on earth may be—whether we toil with the hand, with the brain, or with the heart—we may not bind the soul to any slavish service. Let us do our work like men,—till the soil, build homes, refine brute matter, be learned in law, in medicine, in theology; but let us never chain our souls to what they work in. No earthly work can lay claim to the whole life of man; for every man is born for God, for the Universe, and may not narrow his mind. We must have some practical thing to do in the world,—some way of living which will place us in harmony with the requirements and needs of earthly life; and what this daily business of ours shall be, each one, in view of his endowments and surroundings, must decide for himself.

It is well to bear in mind that every kind of life has its advantages, except an immoral life. Whatever we make of ourselves, then,—whether farmers, mechanics, lawyers, doctors, or priests,—let us above all things first have a care that we are men; and if we are to be men, our special business work must form only a part of our life-work. The aim—at least in this way alone can I look at human life—is not to make rich and successful bankers, merchants, farmers, lawyers, and doctors, but to make noble and enlightened men. Hence the final thought in all work is that we work not to have more, but to be more; not for higher place, but for greater worth; not for fame, but for knowledge. In a word, the final thought is that we labor to upbuild the being which we are, and not merely to build round our real self with marble and gold and precious stones. This is but the Christian teaching which has transformed the world; which declares that it is the business of slaves even, of beggars and outcasts, to work first of all for God and the soul. The end is infinite, the aim must be the highest. Not to know this, not to hear the heavenly invitation, is to be shut out from communion with the best; is to be cut off from the source of growth; is to be given over to modes of thought which fatally lead to mediocrity and vulgarity of life.

> To live for common ends is to be common.
> The highest faith makes still the highest man;
> For we grow like the things our souls believe,
> And rise or sink as we aim high or low.
> No mirror shows such likeness of the face
> As faith we live by of the heart and mind.
> We are in very truth that which we love;
> And love, like noblest deeds, is born of faith.
> The lover and the hero reason not,
> But they believe in what they love and do.
> All else is accident,—this is the soul
> Of life, and lifts the whole man to itself,
> Like a key-note, which, running through all sounds,
> Upbears them all in perfect harmony.

We cannot set a limit to the knowledge and love of man, because they spring from God, and move forever toward him who is without limit. That we have been made capable of this ceaseless approach to an infinite ideal is the radical fact in our nature. Through this we are human; through this we are immortal; through this we are lifted above matter, look through the rippling stream of time on the calm ocean of eternity, and beyond the utmost bounds of space, see simple being,—life and thought and love, deathless, imageless, absolute. This ideal creates the law of duty, for it makes the distinction between right and wrong. Hence the first duty of man is to make himself like God, through knowledge ever-widening, through love ever-deepening, through life ever-growing.

So only can we serve God, so only can we love him. To be content with ignorance is infidelity to his infinite truth. To rest in a lesser love is to deny the boundless charity which holds the heavens together and makes them beautiful, which to every creature gives its fellow, which for the young bird makes the nest, for the child the mother's breast, and in the heart of man sows the seed of faith and hope and heavenly pity.

Ceaseless growth toward God,—this is the ideal, this is the law of human life, proposed and sanctioned alike by Religion, Philosophy, and Poetry. *Dulcissima vita sentire in dies se fieri meliorem.*

Upward to move along a Godward way,
Where love and knowledge still increase,
And clouds and darkness yield to growing day,
Is more than wealth or fame or peace.

No other blessing shall I ever ask.
This is the best that life can give;
This only is the soul's immortal task
For which 't is worth the pain to live.

It is man's chief blessedness that there lie in his nature infinite possibilities of growth. The growth of animals comes quickly to an end, and when they cease to grow they cease to be joyful; but man, whose bodily development even is slow, is capable of rising to wider knowledge and purer love through unending ages. Hence even when he is old,—if he has lived for what is great and exalted,—his mind is clear, his heart is tender, and his soul is glad. Only those races are noble, only those individuals are worthy, who yield without reserve to the power of this impulse to ceaseless progress. Behold how the race from which we have sprung—the Aryan—breaks forth into ever new developments of strength and beauty in Greece, in Italy, in France, in England, in Germany, in America; creating literature, philosophy, science, art; receiving Christian truth, and through its aid rising to diviner heights of wisdom, power, freedom, love, and knowledge.

And so there are individuals—and they are born to teach and to rule—for whom to live is to grow; who, forgetting what they have been, and what they are, think ever only of becoming more and more. Their education is never finished; their development is never complete; their work is never done. From victories won they look to other battlefields; from every height of knowledge they peer into the widening nescience; from all achievements and possessions they turn away toward the unapproachable Infinite, to whom they are drawn. Walking in the shadow of the too great light of God, they are illumined, and they are darkened. This makes Newton think his knowledge ignorance; this makes Saint Paul think his heroic virtue naught. Oh, blessed men, who make us feel that we are of the race of God; who measure and weigh the heavens; who love with boundless love; who toil and are patient; who teach us that workers can wait! They are in love with life; they yearn for fuller life. Life is good, and the highest life is God; and wherever man grows in knowledge, wisdom, and strength, in faith, hope, and love, he walks in the way of heaven.

To you, young gentlemen, who are about to quit these halls, to continue amid other surroundings the work of education which here has but begun, what words shall I more directly speak? If hitherto you have wrought to any purpose, you will go forth into the world filled with resolute will and noble enthusiasm to labor even unto the end in building up the being which is yourself, that you may unceasingly approach the type of perfect manhood. This deep-glowing fervor of enthusiasm for what is highest and best is worth more to you, and to any man, than all that may be learned in colleges. If ambition is akin to pride, and therefore to folly, it is none the less a mighty spur to noble action; and where it is not found in youth, budding and blossoming like the leaves and flowers in spring, what promise is there of the ripe fruit which nourishes life? The love of excellence bears us up on the swift wing and plumes of high desire,—

> Without which whosoe'er consumes his days,
> Leaveth such vestige of himself on earth

As smoke in air or foam upon the wave.

Do not place before your eyes the standard of vulgar success. Do not say, I will study, labor, exercise myself, that I may become able to get wealth or office, for to this kind of work the necessities of life and the tendency of the age will drive you; whereas, if you hope to be true and high, it is your business to hold yourselves above the spirit of the age. It is our worst misfortune that we have no ideals. Our very religion, it would seem, is not able to give us a living faith in the reality of ideals; for we are no longer wholly convinced that souls live in the atmosphere of God as truly as lungs breathe the air of earth. We find it difficult even to think of striving for what is eternal, all-holy, and perfect, so unreal, so delusive do such thoughts seem.

Who will understand that to be is better than to have, and that in truth a man is worth only what he is? Who will believe that the kingdom of this world, not less than the kingdom of Heaven, lies within? Who, even in thinking of the worth of a pious and righteous life, is not swayed by some sort of honesty-best-policy principle? We love knowledge because we think it is power; and virtue, because we are told as a rule it succeeds. Ah! do you love knowledge for itself?—for it is good, it is godlike to know. Do you love virtue for its own sake?—for it is eternally and absolutely right to be virtuous. Instead of giving your thoughts and desires to wealth and position, learn to know how little of such things a true and wise man needs; for the secret of a happy life does not lie in the means and opportunities of indulging our weaknesses, but in knowing how to be content with what is reasonable, that time and strength may remain for the cultivation of our nobler nature. Ask God to inspire you with some great thought, some abiding love of what is excellent, which may fill you with gladness and courage, and in the midst of the labors, the trials, and the disappointments of life, keep you still strong and serene.

Chapter VII.

Right Human Life.

What do we gather hence but firmer faith
That every gift of noble origin
Is breathed upon by Hope's perpetual breath;
That virtue and the faculties within
Are vital, and that riches are akin
To fear, to change, to cowardice, and death?

WORDSWORTH.

What is so delightful as spring weather? To it, whatever mystery life can make plain, it reveals. There is universal utterance. Water leaps from its winding sheet of snow; the streams spring out to wander till they find their source; the corn sprouts to receive the sun's warm kiss; the buds unfold, the blossoms send forth fragrance, the heavens weep for joy; the birds sing, the children shout, and the fuller pulse of life gives, even to the old, fresh thoughts and young desires. Now, what is all this but a symbol of the soul, which feels the urgency of God calling upon it to make itself alive in him and in his universe of truth and beauty?

But the season of growth is also the time of blight. A hundred germs perish for one that ripens into wholesome fruit; a hundred young lives suffer physical or moral ruin for one that develops into some likeness of true manhood. And upon what slight causes success or failure seems to depend!

As a mere word, a glance, will bring the blood to a maiden's cheek, so may it sow the germ of moral death in the heart of youth. How helpless and ignorant the young are in their seeming strength and smartness: how self-sufficient in their unwisdom, how little amenable to reason, how slow to perceive true ideals. What patient, persevering effort is required to form character, and what a little thing will poison life in its source! How easy it is to see and understand what is coarse and evil, how difficult to appreciate what is pure and excellent. How quickly a boy learns to find pleasure in what is animal or brutal; but what infinite pains must be taken before he is won to the love of truth and goodness. Caricature delights him, and he has no eyes for the chaste beauty of perfect art. The story of an outlaw fills him with enthusiasm, and the heroic struggles of godlike souls are for him meaningless. He gazes with envious awe upon some vulgar rich man, and finds a philosopher, or a saint, only queer. He studies because he has been sent to school, where ignorance will expose him to ridicule and humiliation, and possibly too, because he is told that knowledge will help him to win money and influence. However great his proficiency, he is in truth but a barbarian, without wisdom, without reverence, without gentleness. He has been brought only in a vague way into communion with the conscious life of the race; he has no true conception of the dignity of souls, no sense of the beauty of modest and unselfish action. He mistakes rudeness for strength, boastfulness for ability, disrespect for independence, profanity for manliness, brutality for courage.

And to add to his misfortune, he is blind to his own weakness and ignorance. A sneer or a jest is his reply to the voice of wisdom, as with a light heart he walks in the road to ruin; and thus it happens that for one who becomes a true and noble man, a hundred go astray or sink into an unintelligent and vulgar kind of life. This fact is concealed from the eyes of the young, from the eyes of the multitude, indeed. As we hide the dead in the earth that we may quickly forget our loss, so society buries from sight and thought those who fail. Their number is so great that the oblivion which soon overwhelms them is needful to save even the brave from discouragement. Of a hundred college boys the lives of twenty-five will be ruined by dissipation, by sensual indulgence; twenty-five others will be wrecked by unhappy marriages, foolish financial schemes, dishonesty and indolence; of the remaining fifty, forty, let us say, will manage to get on without loss of respectability, while the ten (who are still left) will win a sort of notoriety by getting rich or by getting elected to office. Of the hundred will one become a saint, a philosopher, a poet, a statesman, or even a man of superior ability in natural knowledge or literature? And if this estimate is rightly made they all fail; and the emergence of a high and noble mind is so improbable that it may almost be looked upon, like the birth of a genius, as an accident, so impossible is it, with our limited view, to bring such cases within the domain of law. These hundred college boys have been taken from a thousand youths. The nine hundred have remained outside the doors which open into the halls of culture, away from the special influences which thought and ingenuity have created to develop and perfect man's endowments. As they are less favored, we demand less of them, and are content to have them reinforce the unenlightened army of laborers and money-getters. But when we come among those to whom leisure and opportunity are given that they may learn to think truly and to act nobly, and find that they fail in this, as nearly all of them do fail, we are disappointed and saddened. The thoughtless imagine that those who provide food and shelter do the most important work; but such work is the most important only where there is no intellectual, moral, or religious life. That is most necessary which nourishes the highest faculty, and wherever civilization exists, enlightened minds and great characters are indispensable. The animal and the savage, without much difficulty, find what satisfies appetite; but God appoints that only living souls shall provide what keeps souls alive. Now this soul-life, which manifests itself in thought, in conduct, in hope, faith, and love, makes us human and lifts us above every other kind of earthly existence. It is our distinctive attribute, the godlike side of our being, which, under penalty of sinking to lower worlds, we must bring out and cultivate. The plant is alive. By its own energy it springs from darkness, it grows, it waves its green leaves beneath the blue heavens; but it is blind, deaf and dumb, senseless, dead to the world of sight and sound, of taste and smell. The animal too is alive, and in a higher way: for all the glories of Nature are painted upon its eye; all sounds strike upon its ear; it moves about and has all the sensations of physical pleasure of which man is capable; but it is without thought, without sense of right and wrong, without imagination, without hope and faith. It is plain then that human life, in its highest sense, is life of the soul,—a life of thought and love, of faith and hope, of imagination and desire; and men are high or low as they partake more or less of this true life. By this standard, and by no other, reason requires that we form an estimate of human worth. To be a king, to have money, to live in splendor, to meet with approval from few or many,—is accidental, is something which may happen to an ignorant, a heartless, a depraved, a vulgar man. The most vicious and brutal of men have, again and again, held the most exalted positions, and as a rule cringing and lying, trickery and robbery, or speculation and gambling, have been and are the means by which great fortunes are acquired. Position, then, and money are distinguishable from worth; and they may be and often are found where the life of thought and love, of faith and hope, of imagination and desire, is almost wholly wanting. Now, it is this life—the only true human life—which education should bring forth and strengthen; and the failure to lead this life, of those who pass through our institutions of learning, is a subject of deep concern for all who observe and reflect; for among them we look for the leaders who shall cause wisdom and goodness to prevail over ignorance and appetite. If those who receive the best nurture and care remain on the low plains of a hardly more than animal existence, what hope is there that the multitude shall rise to nobler ways of living?

There is question here of the most vital interests; and if we discover the causes of the evil, a remedy may be found. These causes of failure lie partly in our environment and partly within ourselves. In the home, in which we receive the first and the most enduring impressions, true views and noble aims are frequently wanting; and thus false and low estimates of life are formed at a time when what we learn sinks into the very substance of the mind, and colors and shapes all our future seeing and loving. This primal experience accompanies us, and hangs about us like a mist to shut out the view of fairer worlds. Enthusiasm for intellectual and moral excellence is never roused, because our young souls were not made magnetic by the words and deeds of those whom we looked up to as gods. Fortunate is he who bears with him into the life-struggle pure memories of a happy home. When I think of the bees I have seen coming back to the hive, honey-laden, in the golden light of setting suns, when I was a boy at home, a feeling comes over me as though I had lived in paradise and been driven forth into a bleak world. When one is young, and one's father and mother are full of health and joy; when the roses are blooming and the brooks are laughing to themselves from simple gladness, and the floating clouds and the silent stars seem to have human thoughts,—what more could we ask of God but to know that all this is eternal, and is from him?

In such a mood, how easy it is to turn the childlike soul to the world of spiritual and immortal things. With what efficacy then a mother's soft voice teaches us that we were born upon this earth for no other purpose than to know truth, to love goodness, to do right, that so, having made ourselves godlike, we may forever be with God. And if these high lessons blend in our thought with memories which make home a type of heaven, how shall they not through life be a spur to noble endeavor to accomplish the task thus set us? When great-hearted, high-souled boys go forth to college from homes of intelligence and love, then is there well-founded hope that they shall grow to be wise and helpful men, who know and teach truth, who see and create beauty, who do and make others do what becomes a man. Of hardly less importance is the neighborhood in which our early years are passed, and next to the companionship of the home fireside, a boy's best neighbor is Nature. Well for him shall it be, if, like colts and calves, and all happy young things, he is permitted to breath the wholesome air of woods and fields, to drink from flowing streams, to lie in the shade of trees on the green sward, or to stand alone beneath the silent starlit heavens until the thought and feeling of the infinite and eternal sink deep into his soul, and make it impossible that he should ever look upon the universe of time and space, or the universe of duty's law within his breast, in a shallow or irreverent spirit. Little shall be said to him, and little shall he speak, and to the unobservant he shall seem dull; but he is Nature's nursling, and she paints her colors on his brain and infuses her strength into his heart. She hardens him and teaches him patience; she shows him real things, fills him with the love of truth, and makes him understand that sham is shame.

His progress may be slow; but he will persevere, he will have faith in the power of labor and of time, and when in after years we shall look about for a man with some Diogenes' lantern, there are a thousand chances to one that when we find him we shall find him country-born, not city-bred. Too soon is the town-boy made self-conscious; he is precocious; all the tricks and devices of civilization are known to him; all artifices and contrivances he sees in shop-windows; the street, the theatre, the newspaper are the rivals of the home, and they quickly teach him irreverence and disobedience. He loses innocence, experience of evil gives him flippant views. He becomes wise in his own conceit; having eyes only for the surfaces of things, he easily persuades himself that he knows all. Of such a youth how shall any college make an enlightened, a noble, and a reverent man? But the home and the neighborhood are not our whole environment. As we are immersed in an atmospheric ocean, so do we swim in the current of our national life. To praise this life is easy. We all see and feel how vigorous it is, how confident, how eager. Here is a world of busy men and women, active in many directions. They found States, they build cities, they create wealth, they discuss all problems, they try all experiments, they hurry on to new tasks, and think they have done nothing while aught remains to do.

They live in the midst of the excitement of ever-recurring elections, of speculation, of financial schemes and commercial enterprises. It is an unrestful, feverish, practical life, in which all the strong natures are thinking of doing something, of gaining something,—a life in the market-place, where high thought and noble conduct are all but impossible, where the effort to make one's self a man, instead of striving to get so many thousands of money, would seem ridiculous. It is a life of inventions and manufactures, of getting and spending, in which we bring forth and consume in a single century what it has taken Nature many thousand years to hoard. Our aim is to have more rather than to be more; our ideal is that of material progress; our praise is given to those who invent and discover the means of augmenting wealth. Liberty is opportunity to get rich; education is the development of the money-getting faculty. Our national life may, of course, be looked at from many sides, but the general drift of opinion and effort is in the direction here pointed out. Nine tenths of our thought and energy are given to material interests, and these interests represent nine tenths of our achievements. This may be true of men in general, it may be true also that material progress is a condition of moral and intellectual growth; but none the less is it true that right human life is a life of thought and love, of hope and faith, of imagination and desire. Consequently in a well-ordered society, the chief aim—nine tenths of all effort, let us say—will have for its object the creation of enlightened and loving men and women, whom faith and hope shall make strong, whom imagination shall refresh, and the desire of perfection shall keep active. The aims which the ideals of democracy suggest are not wholly or chiefly material. We strive, indeed, to create a social condition in which comfort and plenty shall be within the reach of all; but the better among us understand that this is but an inferior part of our work, and they take no delight whatever in our great fortunes and great cities. If democracy is the best government, it follows that it is the kind of government which is most favorable to virtue, intelligence, and religion. It is faint praise to say that in America there is more enterprise, more wealth, than elsewhere. What we should strive to make ourselves able to say, is, that there is here a more truly human life, more public and private honesty, purity, sympathy, and helpfulness; more love of knowledge, more perfect openness to light, greater desire to learn, and greater willingness to accept truth than is to be found elsewhere. It should be our endeavor to create a world of which it may be said, there life is more pleasant, beauty more highly prized, goodness held in greater reverence, the sense of honor finer, the recognition of talent and worth completer than elsewhere.

Wealth and population should be considered merely as means, which, if we ourselves do not sink beneath our fortune, we shall use to help us to develop on a vast scale, a nobler, freer, and fairer life than hitherto has ever existed. We Americans have a great capacity for seeing things as they are. A thousand shams and glittering vanities have gone down before our straight-looking eyes; and because such things fail to impress us, we seem to be irreverent. We must look more steadfastly, deeper still, until we clearly perceive and understand that to live for money is to lead a false and vulgar life, to rest with complacency in mere numbers is to have a superficial and unreal mind. To form a right judgment of a people, as of individuals, we must consider what they are; not what they have, except in so far as their possessions are the result of work which at once forms and reveals character. And we must know that work is good only in as much as it helps to make life human,—that is, intelligent, moral and religious. And what we have the right to demand of those to whom we give a higher education is, that they shall body forth these principles in their lives and become leaders in the task of spreading them among the multitude. We demand, first of all, that they become men whose hearts are pure and loving, whose minds are open and enlightened, whose motives are benevolent and generous, whose purposes are high and religious; and if they are such men, it shall matter little to what special pursuits they turn, for whatever their occupation, honor, truth, and intelligence shall go with them, bearing, like mercy, a blessing for those who give and a blessing for those who receive. The spirit in which they work shall be more than what they do, as they themselves shall be more than what they accomplish.

A right spirit transforms the whole man, and the first and highest aim of the educator should be to impart a new heart, a new purpose, which shall bring into play forces that may oppose and overcome those faults of the young of which I have spoken, and which, if not corrected, lead to failure.

And here we come to the causes of ill success which lie within ourselves. We have our individual qualities and defects, and we have also the qualities and defects of the people whence we are sprung, and of the time-spirit into which we are born. It is the aim of education, as it is the aim of religion, to lift us above the spirit of the age; but in attempting to do this, they who lose sight of what is true and beneficent in that spirit, commit a serious blunder.

A national spirit, too, is a narrow, and often a harsh and selfish spirit; but when culture and religion strive to make us citizens of the world and universally benevolent, a care must be had that we retain what is strong and noble in the character we inherit from our ancestors.

The lover of intellectual excellence, however, is little inclined to dwell with complacency either upon his own qualities, or upon the greatness of his country or his age. The untaught optimism which leads the crowd to exaggerate the worth of whatever they in any way identify with themselves, he looks upon with suspicion, if not with aversion. Self-complacency is pleasant; but truth alone is good, and they who think least are best content with themselves and with their world. He who seeks to improve his mind, neither boasts of his age and country, nor rails at them; but tries to understand them as he tries to know himself. The important knowledge here is of obstacles and defects; for when these are removed, to advance is easy. The first lesson which we must learn is that in the work of mental culture, time and patience are necessary elements. The young, who are eager and restless, find it difficult to work with patience and perseverance, especially when the reward of labor is remote, and in the excitement and hurry of American life, such work often seems to be impossible. But by this kind of work alone can true culture be acquired. It is this Buffoon means when he calls genius a great capacity for taking pains. When Albert Dürer said, "Sir, it cannot be better done;" he simply meant that he had bestowed infinite pains upon his work. Now, they who are in a hurry cannot take pains; and they who work for money will take pains only in so far as it is profitable to do so. We must live in our work and love it for its own sake. To do work we love makes us happy, makes us free, and according to its kind educates us; and whatever its kind, it will at least teach us the sovereign virtue of patience, and give us something of the spirit of the old masters who in dingy shops ceased not from labor, and kept their cheerful serenity to the end, though the outcome was only the most perfect fiddle, or a deathless head. But they themselves had the souls of artists, and were honest men, who in their work found joy and freedom, and therefore what they did remains as a source of delight and inspiration. If we find it impossible to put our hearts into our work and consequently impossible to take infinite pains with it, then this is work for which we were not born. The impatient cannot love the labor by which the mind is cultivated, because impatience implies a sense of restraint, a lack of freedom. They are restless, easily grow weary or despondent, find fault with themselves and their task, and either throw off the yoke or bear it in a spirit of disappointment and bitterness. As they fail to make themselves strong and serene, their work bears the marks of haste and feebleness, for work reveals character; it is the likeness of the doer, as style shows the man. Then the young are blinded by the glitter and glare of life, by the splendors of position and wealth; they are drawn to what is external; they would be here and there; they love the unchartered liberty of chance desires, and are easily brought to look upon the task of self-improvement as a slavish work. They would have done with study that they may be free, may enter into what they suppose to be a fair and rich heritage. They cannot understand that so long as they are narrow, sensual, and unenlightened, the possession of a world could not make them high or happy. They do not know that to have liberty, without the power of using it for worthy ends, is a curse not a blessing. They imagine that experience of the world's ways and wickedness will make them wise, whereas it will make them depraved.

How can they realize that the good of life consists in being, and not in having? that we are worth what our knowledge, love, admiration, hope, faith, and desire make us worth? They will not perceive that happiness and unhappiness are conditions of soul, and consequently that the wise, the loving, and the strong, whatever their outward fortune, are happy, while the ignorant, the heartless, and the weak are miserable. To know ourselves, we should seek to discover the kind of life our influence tends to create. Consider the kind of world college boys make for themselves, the things they admire, the companions they find pleasant, the subjects in which they take interest, the books that delight them,—and one great cause of the failure of education will be made plain; for though they are sent to school to be taught by professors, their influence upon one another is paramount. Instead of helping one another to see that their real business is to educate themselves, they persuade one another that life is given for common ends and vulgar pleasures. Hence they look with envy upon their companions who are the sons of rich men, as they have not lived long enough to learn that the fate of four fifths of the sons of rich men in this country, is moral and physical ruin. If such is the public opinion of the world in which they live; and if even strong men are feeble in the presence of public opinion,—how shall we find fault with them for not being attracted by the ideals of intellectual and moral excellence. For the trained mind even to think is difficult, and for them independent thought is almost impossible. They do not know the little less than creative power of right education, or that as we are changed by action, we are transformed by thought. What patient labor may do to exalt and refine the mental faculties, until we become capable of entering into the life of every age and every people, has not been shown to them; and hence they are not inspired by the high hope of dwelling, in very truth, with all the noble and heroic souls who have passed through this world and left record of themselves. We bid the youth learn many things which he cannot but find both useless and uninteresting. And yet unless we discover the secret of winning him to the love of study, the educational value of what he learns is lost; for what leaves him unmoved, leaves him unimproved. His information and accomplishments are comparatively unimportant. What he himself is, and what his real self gives us grounds for hoping he shall become, is the true concern. To be able to translate Æschylus or Plato is not a great thing; but it is a great thing to have the Greek's sense of what is fair, noble and intellectual. To be able to solve a complex mathematical problem may be unimportant; but to have the mental habit of accurate, close, patient thinking is important. It is easy to forget one's Greek or the higher mathematics; but an intellectual or a moral habit is not easily lost.

He who has right habits will go farther and rise higher than he who has only brilliant attainments. It is an error, and a very common one, to suppose that education is merely, or chiefly, a mental process, and consequently that the best school is that in which the various kinds of knowledge are best taught. Our whole being, physical, intellectual, and moral, is subject to the law of education. We may educate the eye, the ear, the hand, the foot; and each member of the body may be trained in many ways. The eye of the microscopist has received a training different from that of the painter; the sculptor's hand has been taught a cunning unlike that of the surgeon; the voice of the orator is developed in one way, that of the singer in another. And so the faculties of the mind may be drawn forth, and each one in various ways. The powers of observation, of reflection, of intuition, of imagination, are all educable. One of the most important and most difficult lessons to learn is that of attention. We know only what we are conscious of, and we are conscious only of that to which we give heed. If we but hold the mind to any subject with perseverance, it will deliver its secret. The little knowledge we have is often vague and unreal, because we are heedless, because we have never taught ourselves to dwell in conscious communion with the objects of thought. The trained eye sees innumerable beauties which are hidden from others, and so the mind which is taught to look right sees truths the uneducated can never know. We may be taught to judge as well as to look. Indeed, once we have learned to see things as they are, correct opinions and judgments naturally follow. All faculty is the result of education. Poets, orators, philosophers, and saints bring not their gifts into the world with them; but by looking and thinking, doing and striving, they rise from the poor elements of half-conscious life to the clear vision of truth and beauty. Natural endowments are not equal; but the chief cause of inequality lies in the unequal efforts which men make to develop their endowments. The lack of imagination in the multitude makes their life dull, uninteresting, and material, and it is assumed that we are born with, or without, imagination, and that there is no remedy for this misery. And those who admit that imagination is subject to the law of development, frequently hold that it should be repressed rather than strengthened. Doubtless the imagination can be cultivated, just as the eye or the ear, the judgment or the reason, can be cultivated; and since imagination, like faith, hope, and love, helps us to live in higher and fairer worlds, an educator is false to his calling when he leaves it unimproved. The classics, and especially poetry, are the great means of intellectual culture, because more than anything else they have power to exalt and ennoble the imagination. To suppose that this faculty is one which only poets and artists need, is to take a shallow and partial view. The historian, the student of Nature, the statesman, the minister of religion, the teacher, the mechanic even, if they are to do good work, must possess imagination, which is at once an intellectual, a moral, and a religious faculty. It is the mother and mistress of faith, hope, and love. It is the source of great thoughts, of high aspirations, and of heavenly dreams. Without it the illimitable starlit expanse loses its sublimity, oceans and mountains their awfulness and majesty, flowers their beauty, home its sacred charm, youth its halo, and the grave its solemn mystery.

Those powers within us which are directly related to conduct, the impulses to self-preservation, and to the propagation of the race, are subject to the law of education, not less than our physical and intellectual endowments. And the importance of dealing rightly with these powers is readily perceived if we reflect that conduct is the greater part of human life, which is a life of thought and love, of hope and faith, of imagination and desire.

As we can educate the faculties of thought and imagination, so can we develop the power to love, to hope, to believe, and to desire. When there is question of the intellect, teachers seek to impart information rather than to strengthen the mind, and when there is question of the moral nature, they have recourse to precepts and maxims instead of striving to confirm the will and to direct impulse. It is generally held, in fact, that will is a gift, not a growth, and the same view is taken of all our moral dispositions. We are supposed to receive from Nature a warm or a cold heart, a hopeful or a despondent temper, a believing or a skeptical turn of mind, a spiritual or a sensual bent. Now as I have already admitted, endowments are unlike; but what has this to do with the drift of the argument? Minds, though by nature unequal, may all be educated; and so wills may be educated, and so that which makes us capable of faith, hope, and desire, may be drawn forth, strengthened, and refined. Emerson, whose thought is predominantly spiritual, takes a low and material view of the moral faculties, confusing strength of will with health. "Courage," he says, "is the degree of circulation of the blood in the arteries.... When one has a plus of health, all difficulties vanish before it." But will is a moral rather than a constitutional power; and in so far as it is moral, it may be cultivated and directed to noble aims and ends. And if the teacher perform this work with fine knowledge and tact, he becomes an educator; for upon the will, more than upon the intellectual faculties, success or failure depends. Whatever we are able to will, we are able to learn to do; and the best service we can render another is to rouse and confirm within him the will to live and to work, that he may make himself a complete man, that thus he may become a benefactor of men and a co-worker with God. The rational will, which is the educated will, should give impulse and guidance to all our thinking, loving, and doing. It should control appetite; it should nourish faith and hope; it should lead us on through the illusory world of sensual delights, through the hardly less illusory world of wealth and power, still bidding us look and see that the world to which the conscious self really belongs, is infinite and eternal, and that to seek to rest in aught else is to apostatize from reason and conscience. Thus it would awaken in us a divine discontent, a sacred unrest, which might urge us on through the darkness of appetite and the unwholesome air of avarice and ambition, whispering to us that our life-work is to know truth, to love beauty, to do righteousness. To none is the education of the will so necessary as to the lovers of intellectual excellence, for they who live in the world of ideas are easily content to let the world of deeds take care of itself. As the astronomer sees the earth lost like a grain of sand in infinite space, so to the wide and deep view of one who is familiar with the course of human thought and action, what any man, what the whole race of man, may do, can seem but insignificant. From the vanity and noise of actors who fret and storm for their brief hour, and then pass forever from life's stage, he flies to ideal worlds where truth never changes, where beauty never grows old, and lives more richly blest than lovers in Tempe or the dales of Arcady. And then the habit of looking at things from many sides leads to doubt, hesitation, and inaction. While the wise deliberate, the young and inexperienced have won or lost the battle. Thus the purely intellectual life tends to weaken faith, hope, and desire, which are the sources whence conduct springs, the drying up of which leaves us amid barren wastes, where high thinking, if it be not impossible, brings neither strength nor joy; for the secret of strength and joy lies in doing and not in thinking. It is a law of our nature that conduct brings the most certain and the most permanent satisfaction, and hence whatever our ideals, the pursuit should be inspired by the sense of duty.

> "Stern law-giver! yet thou dost wear
> The Godhead's most benignant grace;
> Nor know we anything so fair
> As is the smile upon thy face.
> Flowers laugh before thee on their beds
> And fragrance in thy footing treads."

Then only do we move with certain step when we hear God's voice bidding us go forward, as he commands the starry host to fly onward, and all living things to spring upward to light and warmth. When we understand that he has made progress the law of life, we learn to feel that not to grow is not to live. Then our view is enlarged; we become lovers of perfection; we cherish every gift, and in many ways we strive to cultivate the many powers which go to the making of a man. They all are from him, and from him is the effort by which they are improved. We were born to make ourselves alive in him and in his universe, and like the setter in the field, we stretch eye and ear and nose to catch whatever message may be borne to us from his boundless game park. We observe, reflect, compare; we read best books; we listen to whoever speaks what he knows and feels to be truth. We take delight in whatever in Nature is sublime or beautiful, and fresh thoughts and innocent hearts make us glad. Wherever an atom thrills, there too is God, and in him we feel the thrill and are at home. Our faith grows pure; our hope is confirmed; and our love and sympathy identify us with an ever-widening sphere of life beyond us. The exclusive self passes into the larger movement of the social and religious world around us, which, as we now realize, is also within us, giving aims and motives to our love and self-devotion. We understand that what hurts another can never help us, and that our private good must tend to become a general blessing. Thus we find and love ourselves in the intellectual, moral, and religious life of the race, which is a type and symbol of the infinite life of God, the omen and promise of the soul's survival. As we become conscious of ourselves only through communion with what is not ourselves, so we truly live only when we live for God and the world he creates,—losing life that we may find it; dying, like seed-corn, that we may rise to a new and richer life. Not what gratifies our selfish or sensual nature will help us to lead this right human life; but that which illumines and deepens thought and love, which gives to faith a boundless scope, to hope an everlasting foundation, to desire the infinite beauty which, though unseen, is felt, like memory of music fled. The unseen world ceases to be a future world; and is recognized as the very world in which we now think and love, and so intellectual and moral life passes into the sphere of religion. We no longer pursue ideals which forever elude us, but we become partakers of the divine life; for in giving ourselves to the Eternal and Infinite we find God in our souls. The ideal is made real; God is with us, and through faith, hope, and love we are one with him, and all is well. Henceforth in seeking to know more, to become more, we are animated by a divine spirit. Now we may grow old, still learning many things, still smitten with the love of beauty, still finding delight in fresh thoughts and innocent pleasures, and it may be that we shall be found to be teachers of wisdom and of holiness. Then, indeed, shall we be happy, for it is better to teach truth than to win battles. A war-hero supposes a barbarous condition of the race, and when all shall be civilized, they who know and love the most shall be held to be the greatest and the best.

Chapter VIII.

University Education.

As they who look on the ocean think of its vastness; of the many shores in many climes visited by its waves to ply "their priest-like task of clean ablution;" of cities and empires that rose beside its waters, flourished, decayed, and became a memory; of others that shall rise and also pass away, while the moving element remains,—so we to-day beholding ancient Faith, laying, in the New World, the cornerstone of an institution which better than anything else symbolizes the aim and tendency of modern life, find ourselves dwelling in thought upon what has been and what will be.

On the one hand rises the venerable form of that religion whose voice re-echoed in the hearts of Abraham, Moses, David, and Isaiah; whose lips, when the Saviour spoke, uttered diviner truth and thrilled the hearts of men with purer love, living with them in deserts and catacombs, leading them along bloodstained ways to victory and peace, until at length the Church gleamed forth from amid the parting storm-clouds and shone like a mountain-built city bathed in sunlight. On the other stands the Genius of the Republic, the embodied spirit of the sovereign people, who, accepting as literal truth the Christian principles that God is a Father, and men brothers and therefore equal, strive to take from political society the blindness and fatality of natural law, and to endow it with the divine and human attributes of justice, mercy, and intelligence. From the very beginning our American history is full of religious zeal, of high courage and strong endeavor. When Columbus, saddened by the frivolousness or the perfidy of courts, but unshaken in his purpose, walked the streets of the Spanish capital, lonely and forsaken, the children, as he passed along, would point to their foreheads and smile, for was not his mind unhinged, and did he not believe the world was round and on the other side men walked like flies upon a ceiling? But a woman's heart understood that his folly was of the kind which is the wisdom of God, and with her help he set sail, not timidly or doubting like the Portuguese who for fifty years hugged the African coast, advancing and then receding, but facing the awful and untravelled ocean with a heart stronger than its storm-swept billows, he steered due west. In his journal, day after day, he wrote these simple but sublime words, "That day he sailed westward, which was his course." And still, as hope rose and fell, as misgivings and terrors seized on his men, as the compass varied in inexplicable ways as though they were entering regions where the very laws of Nature change, the soul of the great admiral stood firm and each evening he wrote again the self-same words, "that day he sailed westward which was his course," until at length seeing what he foresaw, he gave to Christendom another world and enlarged the boundaries and scope of earthly life. What hearts had not the men who in New England, in Virginia, in Maryland, and elsewhere, settled in little bands on the edge of vast and unexplored regions, covered by interminable forests, where savages lay in wait, athirst for blood. We hear without surprise that wise and prudent men looked upon the early attempts to take possession of America as not less wild and visionary than the legendary exploits of Amadis de Gaul; but what Utopian dreamer, what poet soaring in the high regions of his fancy, could have imagined two centuries and a half ago the beauty, the power, the free and majestic sweep of the stream of human life which has poured across this continent? Who could have dared to hope that the religious exiles who sought here a home for the Christian conscience were a seed, the least of all, which was destined to grow into a tree whose boughs should shelter the land, and bring refreshment to the weary and heavy-laden from every part of the earth?

Who could have thought that these fugitives from the tyrant's power would, in little more than a century, grow like the tribes of Israel into a people able to withstand the onslaughts of the oppressor, and to abolish forever within their borders despotic rule? Who could have had faith that men of different creeds, speaking various tongues, bred in unlike social conditions, would here coalesce and co-operate for the general purposes of free government? Above all, who could have believed that a form of government rarely tried, even in small States, and when tried found practicable only for brief periods, would here become so stable, so strong, that every hamlet, every village, is self-poised and manages its own affairs? The achievement is greater than we are able to know; nor does it lie chiefly in the millions who coming from many lands have here made homes and found themselves free; nor in the building of cities, the clearing of forests, the draining of swamps, the binding of two oceans, and the opening of lines of rapid communication in every direction. Not to numbers or wealth do we owe our significance among the nations; but to the fact that we have shown that respect for law is compatible with civil and religious liberty; that a free people can become prosperous and strong, and preserve order without king or standing army; that the State and the Church can move in separate orbits and still co-operate for the common welfare; that men of different races and beliefs may live together in peace; that in spite of an abnormally rapid increase of population and of wealth, and of the many evils thence resulting, the prevailing tendency is to sanity of thought and sentiment, thus plainly manifesting the vigor of our life and institutions; that the government of the majority, where men put their trust in God and in knowledge, is in the end the government of the good and the wise. We have thus helped to establish confidence in human nature; to prove that man's instincts, like the laws of Nature, are conservative; to show that the enthusiasts who would overturn everything, destroy everything, have no abiding place or influence in the affairs of a free people, as volcanic and cyclonic forces are but transitory and superficial in their action upon the earth. We have shown in a word that under a popular government, where men are faithful and intelligent, it is as impossible that society should become chaotic as that the planets should dissolve into star dust.

It is difficult to realize what an advance this is on all previous views of political life; how full it is of promise, how accordant with the sentiments of the noblest minds in every part of the world. It gives us the leading place among the nations which are moving along rising ways to higher and freer life. To turn to the Catholic Church in America; all observers remark its great development here, the rapid increase in the number of its adherents, its growth in wealth and influence, the firm yet gentle hand with which it brings heterogeneous populations under the control of a common faith and discipline, the ease with which it adapts itself to new conditions and organizes itself in every part of the country. It is not a little thing, in spite of unfriendly public opinion and of great and numerous obstacles, in spite of the burden which high achievements impose and of the lack of easy and supple movement which gathering years imply, to enter new fields, to bend one's self to unaccustomed work, and to struggle for the right to live in the midst of a generation heedless of the good, and mindful only of the evil which has been associated with one's life. This is what the Catholic Church in America has had to do, and has done with a success which recalls the memory of the spread of Christianity through the Roman Empire. It counts its members here by millions, while a hundred years ago it counted them by thousands; and its priests, churches, schools, and institutions of charity it reckons by the thousand, while then they could be counted hardly by tens. Public opinion which was then hostile is no longer so in the same degree. Prejudice has not indeed ceased to exist; for where there is question of religion, of society, of politics, even the fairest minds fail to see things as they are, and the multitude, it may be supposed, will never become impartial; but the tendency of our life and of the age is opposed to bigotry, and as we lose faith in the justice and efficacy of persecution, we perceive more clearly that true religion can neither be defended nor propagated by violence and intolerance, by appeals to sectarian bitterness and national hatred. By none is this more sincerely acknowledged, or more deeply felt, than by the Catholics of the United States.

The special significance of our American Catholic history is not found in the phases of our life which attract attention, and are a common theme for declamation; but it lies in the fact that our example proves that the Church can thrive where it is neither protected nor persecuted, but is simply left to itself to manage its own affairs and to do its work. Such an experiment had never been made when we became an independent people, and its success is of world-wide import, because this is the modern tendency and the position toward the Church which all the nations will sooner or later assume; just as they all will be forced finally to accept popular rule. The great underlying principle of democracy,—that men are brothers and have equal rights, and that God clothes the soul with freedom,—is a truth taught by Christ, is a truth proclaimed by the Church; and the faith of Christians in this principle, in spite of hesitations and misgivings, of oppositions and obstacles and inconceivable difficulties, has finally given to it its modern vigor and beneficent power. The spirit of love and mercy, which is the spirit of Christ, breathes like a heavenly zephyr through the whole earth, and under its influence the age is moved to attempt greater things than hitherto have seemed possible. Never before has sympathy among men been so widespread; never has the desire to come to the relief of all who suffer pain or wrong been so general or so intelligent. To feed the hungry, to clothe the naked, to visit the sick, seems now comparatively a little thing. Our purpose is to create a social condition in which none shall lack food or clothing or shelter; following the divine command: "O Israel, thou shalt not suffer that there be a beggar or a pauper within thy borders." Kindness to slaves ceased to be a virtue for us when we abolished slavery; and we look forward to the day when nor man nor woman nor child shall work and still be condemned to a life of misery. That great blot upon the page of history, woman's fate, has partly been erased, and we are drawing near to the time when in the world as in Christ there shall be made no distinction between slave and freeman, between man and woman. If we compare modern with ancient and mediæval epochs, wars have become less frequent, and in war men have become more humane and merciful.

Increasing knowledge of human life as it is found in the savage, in the barbarian, and in the civilized man, fixes us more unalterably in our belief in the worth of progress. The savage and the barbarian are hopelessly ignorant, and therefore weak and wretched, since ignorance is the chief source of man's misery. "My people," says the prophet, "are destroyed for lack of knowledge." From ignorance rather than from depravity have sprung the most appalling crimes, the most pernicious vices. In darkness of mind men have worshipped senseless material things, have deified every cruel and carnal passion; at the dictate of unenlightened conscience they have oppressed, laid waste, and murdered; for lack of knowledge they have perished in the snows of winter, been wasted by miasmatic air, have fallen victims to famine and pestilence, and have bowed for centuries beneath the degrading yoke of tyranny. Science is a ministering angel. The Jesuits by bringing quinine to the knowledge of civilized man have done more to relieve suffering than all the builders of hospitals. Vaccine has wrought more potently than the all-forgetful love of mothers; more than all the patriots gunpowder has won victories over tyrants; and the printing-press is a greater teacher than philosophers, writers, poets, schools, and universities. Like a heavenly messenger the compass guides man whithersoever he will go, still turning to the one fixed point, as turn the hearts of the children of men to God. The nations intermingle and lose their jealousies and hatreds, borne everywhere by the power of steam; and the thoughts of men are carried by lightning round the whole earth. Commerce has become a world-wide interchange of good offices; and while it adds to the comfort of all, it enlarges thought and strengthens sympathy. Our greater knowledge has enabled us to lengthen human life; to extinguish some of the most virulent diseases; to perform surgical operations without pain; to increase the fertility of the soil; to make pestilential regions habitable; to illumine our cities and homes at night with the brilliancy of day; to give to laborers better clothing and dwellings than princes in other ages have had. It has opened to our vision the limitless sidereal expanse, and revealed to us a heavenly glory which transcends the imagination of inspired poets. Before this new light the earth has dwindled away and become an atom, as the stars hide when the great sun wheels upward from out the night. We have looked into the very heart of the sun itself, and know of what it is made; and with the microscope we have caught sight of the marvellous world of the infinitesimally small, have seen what human eye had never beheld, and have watched unseen life building up and breaking down all living organisms. We have learned how to walk secure in the depths of ocean, to soar in mid-air, to rush on our way unimpeded through the stony hearts of mountains. We see the earth grow from a fire-ball to be the home of man; we know its anatomy; we read its history; and we behold races of animals which passed away ages before the eye of man looked forth upon the boundless mystery and saw the shadow of the presence of the infinite God. Better than the Greeks we know the history of Greece; than the Romans that of Rome. Words that were never written have whispered to us the dreams and hopes of people that perished and left no record; and the more we have learned of the past the more clearly do we perceive how far the present age surpasses all others in knowledge and in power.

The mighty movement by which this development has been caused, has not slackened, but seems each day to gain new force; and the marvellous changes, political, social, moral, intellectual, and physical, which give character to the nineteenth century are but the prelude to a drama which shall make all past achievements of our race appear weak and contemptible. To imagine that our superiority is merely mechanical and material is to fail to see things as they are. Greater individuals may have lived than now are living, but never before has the world been governed with so much wisdom and so much justice; and the power back of our progress is intellectual, moral, and religious. Science is not material. It is the product of intellect and will; and the great founders of modern science, Copernicus, Kepler, Bacon, Descartes, Galileo, Newton, Leibnitz, Ampère, Liebig, Fresnel, Faraday, and Mayer, were Christians. "However paradoxical it may sound," says DuBois-Reymond, "modern science owes its origin to Christianity."

Since the course of events is left chiefly to the direction of natural causes, and since science enables man to bend the stars, the lightning, the winds, and the waves to his purposes, what shall resist the onward march of those who are armed with such power? Since life is a warfare, a struggle, how shall the ignorant and the thoughtless survive in a conflict in which natural knowledge has placed in the hands of the wise forces which the angels may not wield? Since the prosperity of the Church is left subject to human influence, shall the Son of Man find faith on earth when he comes if the most potent instrument God has given to man is abandoned to those who know not Christ? Why should we who reckon it a part of the glory of the Church in the past that she labored to civilize barbarians, to emancipate slaves, to elevate woman, to preserve the classical writings, to foster music, painting, sculpture, architecture, poetry, and eloquence, think it no part of her mission now to encourage scientific research? To be Catholic is to be drawn not only to the love of whatever is good and beautiful, but also to the love of whatever is true; and to do the best work the Catholic Church must fit herself to a constantly changing environment, to the character of every people, and to the wants of each age. Has not Christ declared that whoever is not against us is for us; and may we not therefore find friends in all who work for worthy ends,—for liberty and knowledge, for increase of power and love? This large sympathy, which true religion and the best culture promote, is Catholic, and it is also American; for here with us, I think, the whole world is for men of good-will who are not fools. We who are the children of ancient Faith, who inherit the boon from fathers who held it to be above all price, are saved, where there is question of former times, from irreverent thoughts and shallow views.

For us the long past ages have not flown;
Like our own deeds they travel with us still;
Reviling them, we but ourselves disown;
We are the stream their many currents fill.
From their rich youth our manhood has upgrown,
And in our blood their hopes and loves yet thrill.

But if like the old, the Church can look to the past, like the young, she can look to the future. If there are Catholics who linger regretful amid glories that have vanished, there are also Catholics who in the midst of their work feel a confidence which leaves no place for regret; who well understand that the earthly environment in which the Church lives is subject to change and decay, and that new surroundings imply new tasks and impose new duties. The splendor of the mediæval Church, its worldly power, the pomp of its ceremonial, the glittering pageantry in which its pontiffs and prelates vied with kings and emperors in gorgeous display, are gone, or going; and were it given to man to recall the past, the spirit whereby it lived would still be wanting. But it is the mark of youthful and barbarous natures to have eyes chiefly for the garb and circumstance of religion, to see the body only and not the soul. At all events the course of life is onward, and enthusiasm for the past cannot become the source of great and far reaching action. The present alone gives opportunity; and the face of hope turns to the future, and the wise are busy with what lies at hand, with immediate duty, and not with schemes for bringing back the things that have passed away. Leaving their dead with the dead, they work for life and for the living.

As in each individual there is a better and a worse self, so in each age there are conflicting tendencies; but it is the part of enlightened minds and generous hearts to see what is true, and to love what is good. The fault-finder is hateful both in life and in literature; and it is Iago, the most despicable of characters, whom Shakespeare makes say, "I am nothing if not critical." A Christian of all men is without excuse for being fretful and sour, for thinking and acting as though this were a devil's world, and not the eternal God's, as though there were danger lest the Almighty should not prevail. We know that God is, and therefore that all will be well; and if it were conceivable that God is not, it would still be the part of a true man to labor to make knowledge and virtue prevail. The criticism of the age which gives a better understanding of its needs is good; all other is baneful.

Opinion rules the world, and a right appreciation of the influences by which opinion is moulded is the surest guide to a knowledge of the time. In ignorant and barbarous ages the notions and beliefs of men are crude, and are controlled by a few, for only a few possess knowledge and influence; and even in the age of Pericles and Augustus, the thought of mankind means the thoughts of some dozens of men. A few vigorous minds founded schools of opinion and style, became intellectual dictators, and asserted their authority for centuries. As the art of printing was yet unknown, and books were rare, the teacher was the speaker; orators held sway over the destiny of nations; and the Christian pulpit became the world's university. But the printing-press in giving to thought a permanent form which is placed under the eyes of the whole world has made the passion, the splendor, the majestic phrase of oratory seem unreal as an actor's speech, evanescent as a singer's tones; and hence the pulpit and the rostrum, though they still have influence, can never again exercise the control over opinion which belonged to them when all men had not become readers.

What is true of eloquence may be affirmed of all art. In spite of ourselves, even the best of us find it difficult to make art a serious business; and unless taken seriously, it is vain, loses its soul, and falls into the hands of pretenders and sentimentalists. Once painting, sculpture, architecture, and song were the expression of thoughts and moods which irresistibly appealed for utterance; but with us they are a fashion, like cosmetics and laces. Poetry, the highest of arts, has lost its original character of song, and the poet now deals, in an imaginative way, with problems which puzzle metaphysicians and theologians. The causes that have robbed art of so much of its charm and power have necessarily diminished the influence of ceremonial worship, which is the artistic expression of the soul's faith and love, of its hopes and yearnings. We are, indeed, still subdued by the majesty of dimly lighted cathedrals, by solemn music, and the various symbolism of the ritual, but we feel not the deep awe of our fathers whose knees furrowed the pavement stones, and whose burning lips kissed them smooth; and to blame ourselves for this would serve no purpose. To those who find no pleasure in sweet sounds, we pipe in vain, and argument to show that one ought to be moved by what leaves him cold, is meaningless. Emotion is spontaneous, and adorers, like lovers, neither ask nor care for reasons. There is in fact an element of illusion in feeling; passion is non-rational; and when the spirit of the time is intellectual, men are seldom devout, however religious they may be. The scientific habit of mind is not favorable to childlike and unreasoning faith; and the new views of the physical universe which the modern mind is forced to take, bring us face to face with new problems in religion and morals, in politics and society.

Whatever we may think of the past, whatever we may fear or hope for the future, if we would make an impression on the world around us, we must understand the thoughts, the purposes, and the methods of those with whom we live; and we must at the same time recognize that though the truth of religion be unchangeable, the mind of man is not so, and that the point of view varies not only from people to people, and from age to age, but from year to year in the growing thought of the individual and of the world. As in travelling round the earth, time changes, and when it is morning here, it is evening there, so with difference of latitude and longitude, of civilization and barbarism, the opinions and manners of men grow different. They who observe from positions widely separate do not see the same things, or do not see them in the same light. Proof for a peasant is not proof for a philosopher; and arguments which in one age are held to be unanswerable, in another lose power to convince, or become altogether meaningless. It is not to be imagined that the hearts of Christians should again burn with the devotional enthusiasm and the warlike ardor of the Crusaders; and just as little is it conceivable that men should again become passionately interested in the questions which in the fourth and fifth centuries filled the world with the noise of theological disputation. It were mere loss of time to beat now the waste fields of the Protestant controversy. Wiseman's book on science and revealed religion, which fifty years ago attracted attention, lies like a stranded ship on a deserted shore, and attempts of the kind are held in slight esteem. The immature mind is eager to reduce faith to knowledge; but the accomplished thinker understands that knowledge begins and ends in faith. There is oppugnancy between belief in an all-wise, all-good, and all-powerful God, and belief in the divine origin of Nature, whose face is smeared with filth and blood; but we hold that the conflicting faiths and increasing knowledge cannot add to the difficulty. On the contrary, the higher the intelligence, the purer Nature seems to grow. The chemical elements are as fair and sweet in the corpse as in the living body, and the earthquake and the cyclone obey the same laws which make the waters flow and the zephyrs breathe perfume. It is the imagination and not the reason that is overwhelmed by the idea of unending space and time. To the intellect, eternity is not more mysterious than the present moment, and the distance which separates us from the remotest stars is not more incomprehensible than a hand's breadth. Science is the widening thought of man, working on the hypothesis of universal intelligibility toward universal intelligence; and religion is the soul, escaping from the labyrinth of matter to the light and love of the Infinite; and on the heights they meet and are at peace.

Meanwhile they who seek natural knowledge must admit that faith, hope, and love are the everlasting foundations of human life, and that a philosophic creed is as sterile as Platonic love; and they who uphold religion must confess that faith which ignorance alone can keep alive is little better than superstition. To strive to attain truth under whatever form is to seek to know God; and yet no ideal can be true for man, unless it can be made to minister to faith, hope, and love; for by them we live. Let us then teach ourselves to see things as they are, without preoccupation or misgivings lest what is should ever make it impossible, for us to believe and hope in the better yet to be. Science and morality need religion as much as thought and action require emotion; and beyond the utmost reach of the human mind lie the boundless worlds of mystery where the soul must believe and adore what it can but dimly discern. The Copernican theory of the heavens startled believers at first; but we have long since grown accustomed to the new view which reveals to us a universe infinitely more glorious than aught the ancients ever imagined. We do not rightly see either the things which are always around us, or those which for the first time are presented to our eyes; and when novel theories of the visible world, which in some sense is part of our very being, profoundly alter our traditional notions, the mind is disturbed and overclouded, and the lapse of time alone can make plain the real bearing of the new learning upon life, upon religion, and upon society. There can be no doubt but increase of knowledge involves incidental evils, just as the progress of civilization multiplies our wants; but the wise are not therefore driven to seek help from ignorance and barbarism. Whatever the loss, all knowledge is gain. The evils that spring from enlightenment of mind will find their remedy in greater enlightenment. Such at least is the faith of an age whose striking characteristic is confidence in education. Men have ceased to care for the bliss there may be in ignorance, and those who dread knowledge, if such there still be, are as far away from the life of this century as the dead whose bones crumbled to dust a thousand years ago.

The aim the best now propose to themselves is to provide not wealth or pleasure, or better machinery or more leisure, but a higher and more effective kind of education; and hence whatever one's preoccupation, whether social, political, religious, or industrial, the question of education forces itself upon his attention. Pedagogy has grown to be a science, and chairs are founded in universities to expound the theory and art of teaching. The learning of former times has become the ignorance of our own; and the classical writings have ceased to be the treasure-house of knowledge, and in consequence their educational value has diminished.

Whoever three hundred years ago wished to acquaint himself with philosophic, poetic, or eloquent expression of the best that was known, was compelled to seek for it in the Greek and Latin authors; but now Greek and Latin are accomplishments chiefly, and a classical scholar, if unacquainted with modern science and literature, is hopelessly ignorant. "If any one," said Hegius, the teacher of Erasmus, "wishes to learn grammar, rhetoric, mathematics, history, or holy scripture, let him read Greek;" and in his day this was as true as it is false and absurd in our own. In the Middle Ages,

Latin was made the groundwork of the educational system, not on account of any special value it may have been supposed to possess as a mental discipline, but because it was the language of the learned, of all who spoke or wrote on questions of religion, philosophy, literature, and science; but now, who that is able to think dreams of burying his thought in a Greek or Roman urn? The Germans in philosophy, the English in poetry, have surpassed the Greeks; and French prose is not inferior in qualities of style to the ancient classics, and in wealth of thought and knowledge so far excels them as to preclude comparison.

The life of Greece and Rome, compared with ours, was narrow and superficial; their ideas of Nature were crude and often grotesque; they lacked sympathy; the Greek had no sense of sin; the Roman none of the mercy which tempers justice. In their eyes the child was not holy, woman was not sacred, the slave was not man. Their notion of liberty was political and patriotic merely; the human soul, standing forth alone, and appealing from States and emperors to the living God, was to them a scandal. Now literature is the outgrowth of a people's life and thought, and the nobler the life, the more enlightened the thought, the more valuable will the expression be; and since there is greater knowledge, wisdom, freedom, justice, mercy, goodness, power, in Christendom now than ever existed in the pagan world, it would certainly be an anomaly if modern literature were inferior to the classical. The ancients, indeed, excel us in the sense for form and symmetry. There is also a freshness in their words, a joyousness in their life, a certain heroic temper in their thinking and acting, which give them power to engage the emotions; and hence to deny them exceptional educational value is to take a partial view. But even though we grant that the study of their literatures is in certain respects the best intellectual discipline, education, it must be admitted, means knowledge as well as training; and thorough training is something more than refined taste. It is strength as well, and ability to think in many directions and on many subjects. Nothing known to men should escape the attention of the wise; for the knowledge of the age determines what is demanded of the scholar. And since it is our privilege to live at a time when knowledge is increasing more rapidly even than population and wealth, we must, if we hope to stand in the front ranks of those who know, keep pace with the onward movement of mind. To turn away from this outburst of splendor and power; to look back to pagan civilization or Christian barbarism,—is to love darkness more than light. Aristotle is a great mind, but his learning is crude and his ideas of Nature are frequently grotesque.

Saint Thomas is a powerful intellect; but his point of view in all that concerns natural knowledge has long since vanished from sight. What poverty of learning does not the early mediæval scheme of education reveal; and when in the twelfth century the idea of a university rises in the best minds, how incomplete and vague it is! Amid the ruins of castles and cathedrals we grow humble, and think ourselves inferior to men who thus could build. But they were not as strong as we, and they led a more ignorant and a blinder life; and so when we read of great names of the past, the mists of illusion fill the skies, and our eyes are dimmed by the glory of clouds tinged with the splendors of a sun that has set.

Certainly a true university will be the home both of ancient wisdom and of new learning; it will teach the best that is known, and encourage research; it will stimulate thought, refine taste, and awaken the love of excellence; it will be at once a scientific institute, a school of culture, and a training ground for the business of life; it will educate the minds that give direction to the age; it will be a nursery of ideas, a centre of influence. The good we do men is quickly lost, the truth we leave them remains forever; and therefore the aim of the best education is to enable students to see what is true, and to inspire them with the love of all truth. Professional knowledge brings most profit to the individual; but philosophy and literature, science and art, elevate and refine the spirit of the whole people, and hence the university will make culture its first aim, and its scope will widen as the thoughts and attainments of men are enlarged and multiplied. Here if anywhere shall be found teachers whose one passion is the love of truth, which is the love of God and of man; who look on all things with a serene eye; who bring to every question a calm, unbiased mind; who, where the light of the intellect fails, walk by faith and accept the omen of hope; who understand that to be distrustful of science is to lack culture, to doubt the good of progress is to lack knowledge, and to question the necessity of religion is to want wisdom; who know that in a God-made and God-governed world it must lie in the nature of things that reason and virtue should tend to prevail, in spite of the fact that in every age the majority of men think foolishly and act unwisely. How divine is not man's apprehensive endowment! When we see beauty fade, the singer lose her charm, the performer his skill, we feel no commiseration; but when we behold a noble mind falling to decay, we are saddened, for we cannot believe that the godlike and immortal faculty should be subject to death's power. It is a reflection of the light that never yet was seen on sea or land; it is the magician who shapes and colors the universe, as a drop of water mirrors the boundless sky. Is not this the first word the Eternal speaks?—"Let there be light." And does not the blessed Saviour come talking of life, of light, of truth, of joy, and peace? Have not the Christian nations moved forward following after liberty and knowledge? Is not our religion the worship of God in spirit and in truth? Is not its motive Love, divine and human, and is not knowledge Love's guide and minister?

The future prevails over the present, the unseen over what touches the senses only in high and cultivated natures; and it is held to be the supreme triumph of God over souls when the young, to whom the earth seems to be heaven revealed and made palpable, turn from all the beauty and contagious joy to seek, to serve, to love Him who is the infinite and only real good. Yet this is what we ask of the lovers of intellectual excellence, who work without hope of temporal reward and without the strength of heart which is found in obeying the Divine Will; for mental improvement is seldom urged as a religious duty, although it is plain that to seek to know truth is to seek to know God, in whom and through whom and by whom all things are, and whose infinite nature and most awful power may best be seen by the largest and most enlightened mind. Mind is Heaven's pioneer making way for faith, hope, and love, for higher aims and nobler life; and to doubt its worth and excellence is to deny the reasonableness of religion, since belief, if not wholly blind, must rest on knowledge. The best culture serves spiritual and moral ends. Its aim and purpose is to make reason prevail over sense and appetite; to raise man not only to a perception of the harmonies of truth, but also to the love of whatever is good and fair. Not in a darkened mind does the white ray of heavenly light break into prismatic glory; not through the mists of ignorance is the sweet countenance of the divine Saviour best discerned. If some have pursued a sublime art frivolously; have soiled a fair mind by ignoble life,—this leaves the good of the intellect untouched. Some who have made strongest profession of religion, who have held high and the highest places in the Church, have been unworthy, but we do not thence infer that the tendency of religion is to make men so. They who praise the bliss and worth of ignorance are sophists. Stupidity is more to be dreaded than malignity; for ignorance, and not malice, is the most fruitful cause of human misery. Let knowledge grow, let truth prevail. Since God is God, the universe is good, and the more we know of its laws, the plainer will the right way become. The investigator and the thinker, the man of culture and the man of genius, cannot free themselves from bias and limitation; but the work they do will help me and all men.

Indifference or opposition to the intellectual life is but a survival of the general anti-educational prejudices of former ages. It is also a kind of envy, prompting us to find fault with whatever excellence is a reproach to our unworthiness. The disinterested love of truth is a rare virtue, most difficult to acquire and most difficult to preserve. If knowledge bring power and wealth, if it give fame and pleasure, it is dear to us; but how many are able to love it for its own sake? Do not nearly all men strive to convince themselves of the truth of those opinions which they are interested in holding? What is true, good, or fair is rarely at once admitted to be so; but what is practically useful men quickly accept, because they live chiefly in the world of external things, and care little for the spiritual realms of truth and beauty. The ignorant do not even believe that knowledge gives power and pleasure, and the educated, except the chosen few, value it only for the power and pleasure it gives. As the disinterested love of truth is rare, so is perfect sincerity. Indeed, insincerity is here the radical vice. Good faith is essential to faith; and a sophistical mind is as immoral and irreligious as a depraved heart. Let a man be true, seek and speak truth, and all good things are possible; but when he persuades himself that a lie may be useful and ought to be propagated, he becomes the enemy of his own soul and the foe of all that makes life high and godlike.

Now, to be able to desire to see things as they are, whatever their relations to ourselves may be, and to speak of them simply as they appear to us, is onc result of the best training of the intellect, which in the world of thought and opinion gives us that sweet indifference which is the rule of saints when they submit the conduct of their lives wholly to divine guidance. Why should he whose mind is strong, and rests on God, be disturbed? It is with opinion as with life. We cannot tell what moment truth will overthrow the one and death the other; but thought cannot change the nature of things. The clouds dissolve, but the eternal heavens remain. Over the bloodiest battlefields they bend calm and serene, and trees drink the sunlight and flowers exhale perfume. The moonbeam kisses the crater's lip. Over buried cities the yellow harvest waves, and all the catastrophes of endless time are present to God, who dwells in infinite peace. He sees the universe and is not troubled, and shall not we who are akin to him learn to look upon our little meteorite without losing repose of mind and heart? Were it not a sweeter piety to trust that he who made all things will know how to make all things right; and therefore not to grow anxious lest some investigator should find him at fault or thwart his plans? As living bodies are immersed in an invisible substance which feeds the flame of life, so souls breathe and think and love in the atmosphere of God, and the higher their thought and love the more do they partake of the divine nature. Many things, in this age of transition, are passing away; but true thoughts and pure love are immortal, and whatever opinions as to other things a man may hold, all know that to be human is to be intelligent and moral, and therefore religious. A hundred years hence our present machinery may seem to be as rude as the implements of the middle age look to us, and our political and social organization may appear barbarous,—so rapid has the movement of life become. But we do not envy those who shall then be living, partly it may be because we can have but dim visions of the greater blessings they shall enjoy, but chiefly because we feel that after all the true worth of life lies in nothing of this kind, but in knowing and doing, in believing and loving; and that it would not be easier to live for truth and righteousness were electricity applied to aerial navigation and all the heavens filled with argosies of magic sail. It is not possible to love sincerely the best thoughts, as it is not possible to love God when our aim is something external, or when we believe that what is mechanical merely has power to regenerate and exalt mankind.

> "It takes a soul
> To move a body; it takes a high-souled man
> To move the masses ... even to a cleaner sty;
> It takes the ideal to blow a hair's-breadth off
> The dust of the actual—Ah, your Fouriers failed,
> Because not poets enough to understand
> That life develops from within."

He who believes in culture must believe in God; for what but God do we mean when we talk of loving the best thoughts and the highest beauty? No God, no best; but at most better and worse. And how shall a man's delight in his growing knowledge not be blighted by a hidden taint, if he is persuaded that at the core of the universe there is only blind unconscious force? But if he believe that God is infinite power working for truth and love, then can he also feel that in seeking to prepare his mind for the perception of truth and his heart for the love of what is good and fair, he is working with God, and moves along the way in which his omnipotent hand guides heavenly spirits and all the countless worlds. He desires that all men should be wiser and stronger and more loving, even though he should be doomed to remain as he is, for then they would have power to help him. He is certain of himself, and feels no fear nor anger when his opinions are opposed. He learns to bear what he cannot prevent, knowing that courage and patience make tolerable immedicable ills. He feels no self-complacency, but rather the self-dissatisfaction which comes of the consciousness of possessing faculties which he can but imperfectly use. And this discontent he believes to be the infinite God stirring within the soul. As the earthquake which swallows some island in another hemisphere disturbs not the even tenor of our way, so the passions of men whose world is other than his, who dwell remote from what he contemplates and loves, shake not his tranquil mind. While they threaten and pursue, his thought moves in spheres unknown to them. He knows how little life at the best can give, and is not hard to console for the loss of anything. There is no true thought which he would not gladly make his own, even though it should be the watchword of his enemies. Since morality is practical truth, he understands that increasing knowledge will make it at once more evident and more attractive. Hatred between races and nations he holds to be not less unchristian than the hatred which arms the individual against his fellow-man. It is impossible for him to be a scoffer; for whatever has strengthened or consoled a human soul is sacred in his eyes; and wherever there is question of what is socially complex, as of a religion or a civilization, there is question of many human lives, their hopes, their joys, their strivings, their yearnings, disappointments, agonies, and deaths; and he is able to perceive that in the ports of levity there is no refuge for hearts that mourn. Does not love itself, in its heaven of bliss, turn away from him who mocks? The lover of the intellectual life knows neither contempt nor indignation, is not elated by success or cast down by failure; money cannot make him rich, and poverty helps to make him free. His own experience teaches him that men in becoming wiser will become nobler and happier; and this sweet truth has in his eyes almost the elements of a religion. With growing knowledge his power of sympathy is enlarged; until like Saint Francis, he can call the sun his brother and the moon his sister; can grieve with homeless winds, and feel a kinship with the clod. The very agonies by which his soul has been wrung open to his gaze visions of truth which else he had never caught, and so he finds even in things evil some touch of goodness. Praise and blame are for children, but to him impertinent. He is tolerant of absurdity because it is so all-pervading that he whom it fills with indignation can have no repose. While he labors like other men to keep his place in the world, he strives to make the work whereby he maintains himself, and those who cling to him, serve intellectual and moral ends. He has a meek and lowly heart, and he has also a free and illumined mind, and a soul without fear. He knows that no gift or accomplishment is incompatible with true religion; for has not the Church intellects as many-sided and as high as Augustine and Chrysostom, Dante and Calderon, Descartes and Da Vinci, De Vega and Cervantes, Bossuet and Pascal, Saint Bernard and Gregory the Seventh, Aquinas and Michael Angelo, Mozart and Fénelon? Ah! I behold the youthful throng, happier than we, who here, in their own sweet country,—in this city of government and of law with its wide streets, its open spaces, its air of freedom and of light,—undisturbed by the soul-depressing hum of commerce and the unintellectual din of machinery, shall hearken to the voice of wisdom and walk in the pleasant ways of knowledge, alive, in every sense, to catch whatever message may come to them from God's universe; who, as they are drawn to what is higher than themselves, shall be drawn together, like planets to a sun; whose minds, aglow with high thinking, shall taste joy and delight fresher and purer than merriest laughter ever tells. Who has not seen, when leaden clouds fill the sky and throw gloomy shadows on the earth, some little meadow amid the hills, with its trees and flowers, its grazing kine and running brook, all bathed in sunlight, and smiling as though a mother said, Come hither, darling?

Such to my fancy is this favored spot, whose invitation is to the fortunate few who believe that "the noblest mind the best contentment has," and that the fairest land is that which brings forth and nurtures the fairest souls. When youthful friends drift apart, and meet again after years, they find they have been living not only in different cities, but in different worlds. Those who shall come up to the university must turn away from much the world holds dear; and while the companions they leave behind shall linger in pleasant places or shall get money, position, and applause, they must move on amid ever-increasing loneliness of life and thought. Xanthippe would have had altogether a better opinion of Socrates had he not been a philosopher, and the best we do is often that for which our age and our friends care the least; but they who have once tasted the delights of a cultivated mind would not exchange them for the gifts of fortune, and to have beheld the fair face of wisdom is to be forever her votary. Words spoken for the masses grow obsolete; but what is fit to be heard by the chosen few shall be true and beautiful while such minds are found on earth. In the end, it is this little band—this intellectual aristocracy—who move and guide the world. They see what is possible, outline projects, and give impulse, while the people do the work. That which is strongest in man is mind; and when a mind truly vigorous, open, supple, and illumined reveals itself, we follow in its path of light. How it may be I do not know; but the very brain and heart of genius throbs forever in the words on which its spirit has breathed. Let this seed, though hidden like the grain in mummy pits for thousands of years, but fall on proper soil, and soon the golden harvest shall wave beneath the dome of azure skies; let but some generous youth bend over the electric page, and lo! all his being shall thrill and flame with new-born life and light. Genius is a gift. But whoever keeps on doing in all earnestness something which he need not do, and for which the world cares hardly at all, if he have not genius, has at least one of its chief marks; and it is, I think, an important function of a university to create an intellectual atmosphere in which the love of excellence shall become contagious, which whosoever breathes shall, like the Sibyl, feel the inspiration of divine thoughts.

Sweet home! where Wisdom, like a mother, shall lead her children in pleasant ways, and to their thoughts a touch of heaven lend! From thee I claim for my faith and my country more blessings than I can speak,—

Our scattered knowledges together bind;
Our freedom consecrate to noble aims.
To music set the visions of the mind;
Give utterance to the truth pure faith proclaims.
Lead where the perfect beauty lies enshrined,
Whose sight the blood of low-born passion tames.

And now, how shall I more fittingly conclude than with the name of her whose generous heart and enlightened mind were the impulse which has given to what had long been hope deferred and a dreamlike vision, existence and a dwelling-place,—Mary Gwendolen Caldwell.

THE END.

Printed by Libri Plureos GmbH in Hamburg,
Germany